Cooking Out
of the Box

Cooking Out of the Box

The Easy Way to Turn
Prepared Convenience Foods into
Delicious Family Meals

BEV BENNETT

PRIMA PUBLISHING

Published by Prima Publishing, Roseville, California. Member of the Crown Publishing Group, a division of Random House, Inc., New York.

PRIMA PUBLISHING and colophon are trademarks of Random House, Inc., registered with the United States Patent and Trademark Office.

Interior illustrations by Sheryl Dickert.

Library of Congress Cataloging-in-Publication Data
Bennett, Bev.
    Cooking out of the box : the easy way to turn prepared convenience foods into delicious family meals / Bev Bennett
        p.   cm.
    Includes index.
    ISBN 0-7615-6359-8
    1. Cookery. 2. Convenience foods. I. Title.
TX714.B389   2002
641.5—dc21   2002074983

02 03 04 05 06 QQ 10 9 8 7 6 5 4 3 2 1
Printed in the United States of America

First Edition

Visit us online at www.primapublishing.com

Hugs and kisses to my husband, Linn, and my children, Ben and Rebecca, who always have ready appetites and keen palates.

CONTENTS

ACKNOWLEDGMENTS

When I needed to bounce food ideas off an audience, the "jugglers" of the www.freelancesuccess.com message boards were there. Thanks for all of your input and support.

To Harry Balzer and the folks at the NPD Group, keep up those reports on what America is actually eating. I appreciate the reality check.

Big chocolate kisses to Grace Freedson for being a great agent and friend with superior listening abilities.

And to Jamie Miller and Michelle McCormack at Prima Publishing, I'm glad you gave me the opportunity to do this book. Thank you both.

Somewhere between finishing off a deadline report, picking up the laundry, and getting the dog to the vet, you forgot to have a meal. Oh sure, you ate. Maybe it was a "nutrition bar" that tasted like chocolate-covered cardboard or a fast-food burger and salty fries that had been sitting on a steam table waiting for your order.

And just imagine, your food habits may get even more frenzied in the future. Scientists are creating cans that heat up as you press a button so that you can sip hot soup while you drive. Futurists envision you in a car with a built-in microwave oven so you can zap as you zip along the freeway. Why, you may never have to sit down to dinner again.

But that's not what you want. Surely you crave the comfort, camaraderie, and sociability of a meal shared with friends and family.

No doubt your childhood memories, like mine, are filled with kitchen scenes. We didn't have a rec room. The kitchen was the hub of our house. After school, my brother and I took turns stirring a pot of chocolate pudding while describing our day to Mom. Sunday evenings, we made popcorn to snack on while watching television.

The dinner table was Mom's strategic command center. We made our summer vacation plans while asking for seconds of barley soup. The fact that it was January in Chicago made both the soup and the anticipated respite from the cold so much more appealing.

I remember announcing my grades when we sat down to dinner. If I had a stellar report card, I passed it around at the beginning of the meal; if it was disappointing, I waited until after dessert. I didn't want to risk having Mom's cheesecake withheld.

Although I can't imagine my parents read surveys on the subject, families that eat together have children who eat more fruits and vegetables and are less likely to have weight problems, say researchers at the Baylor College of Medicine in Houston.

Children who eat as part of a family are less likely to be picky eaters. Did you ever hear the expression "I'm not running a restaurant"? In thousands of households, that translates to "eat what's on the table or go hungry."

The experts are finding powerful psychological benefits to eating meals together. Children have improved school performance, fewer behavioral problems, and certainly better manners.

Eating together as a family is also a strong drug deterrent. A 1999 survey indicated that teens from families that almost always eat dinner together are 31 percent less likely to smoke, drink alcohol, or use illegal drugs, according to the National Center on Addiction and Substance Abuse at Columbia University in New York City.

Unfortunately, cooking is more challenging than it was a generation ago. Although our mothers and grandmothers had a million errands on their agendas, they were usually in the kitchen in the afternoon putting a pot of soup on the stove or getting the roast into the oven. No longer. Many of us aren't home for 12-hour stretches. We don't work a pot roast schedule.

However, we're not about to give up the satisfaction we get from sitting down to a meal with our family. Nor do we want our family to forgo the pleasure of home-cooked food. What can match the smile on a child's face as he or she comes into the kitchen lured by the aroma of a fresh-from-the-oven cake? Trust me—a bag of warmed-over burgers isn't a child magnet.

So, to those doomsayers who would label cooks as the dinosaurs of the kitchen, I say nonsense. We may have been sidetracked for a few years but definitely not vanquished. A cooking revolution is at hand, and it's been documented. We are cooking again. The number of meals Americans prepared at home increased in 2000 for the first time in nearly a decade, according to the NPD Group, Inc., a marketing information firm. The 2000 survey, NPD's most recent one, shows that people are cutting back on restaurant and take-out meals.

What makes this reaffirmation of cooking possible when we're so time crunched? It's the dramatic proliferation of meal products available to consumers. We're seeing a convergence of convenience and familiar home-style ingredients on supermarket shelves.

It was just a few years ago that the poultry industry created cooked, seasoned chicken breast meat. The beef and pork producers were quick to catch up. In case you haven't seen it—or had the wonderful advantage of cooking with it—let me introduce you to the most deliciously convenient product on the market. In your local grocery store, a few steps away from the raw meat and poultry, you'll now find—in boxes—precooked ground beef, barbecued shredded pork, grilled baby back ribs, hamburger patties, chicken, and even pot roasts and stews. Just open a package, heat it up in the microwave or throw it in a pan with other ingredients, and it's ready to go! Add a side of green beans to an out-of-the-box pot roast and you've got the meal your mom made.

Some items require your finishing touches at home. A box of mashed potatoes, for example, comes alive with a little butter and milk. You transform a packet of seasonings into a robust Asian dressing with the addition of oil and vinegar.

If you're culinarily inept (and don't be embarrassed, as most of us claim some weakness in the kitchen), you'll be relieved that the food industry is eliminating most obstacles to cooking. You say you hate to wash salad greens? You don't have to. Open a bag of mixed greens, pour into a bowl, and you've got a nutritious salad.

As you explore the wealth of available food products, you'll notice ways in which you can personalize dishes to suit your family's tastes. Just as you add a favorite piece of jewelry or a scarf to a suit, you can add your preferred spices, herbs, and vegetables to packaged foods.

This book shows you how to harness the speed of ready-made boxed or packaged foods to create wholesome meals and snacks for your family. You'll learn what to stock for almost instant menus for entertaining, and you'll have a recipe treasury that anyone in the house can follow.

With *Cooking Out of the Box*, you'll never again be too time starved to nourish yourself or your family.

stocking the "out of the box" kitchen

I create recipes for a living, so you'd think I never panic at dinner time. Not so. I've had business meetings run late, meat that didn't thaw according to my timetable, and a schedule of children's activities that would wipe the smile off Mary Poppins.

The dinner hour made me so snarly that my family ducked for cover. I was trying to reproduce the idealized dinners of another generation while carrying on a three- or four-way conversation and doing all this while needing to refuel. Something had to give. Clearly my cooking style wasn't satisfying my needs or those of my family.

I realized I had to let go of the idea of cooking everything from scratch. It wasn't even a valid notion. After all, I wasn't making my own spaghetti from flour and water, so why did it matter whether the pasta sauce came from fresh tomatoes or a jar of my supermarket's finest?

I began to explore convenience foods.

My goal wasn't to replace home-cooked foods with zap-heat-and-eat dinners. As corny as it seems, I still yearned to add my own touch. You can bet food manufacturers have caught on as well. They know what they're doing when they leave the eggs out of the cake mix. We all want to add something of our own when we cook.

Instead, I looked for ways to save time. For example, I doctored a packet of Alfredo sauce for a favorite pasta casserole. And I have to admit, the dish was as good tasting as my from-scratch Parmesan cheese sauce. My version of Country Captain, a Southern skillet dish of chicken in a curry-seasoned tomato sauce, took more than an hour to make. When I discovered I could replicate the flavors using a soup mix, a box of cooked chicken meat, and instant rice, I whittled the preparation time to under 20 minutes.

What's more, as I incorporated box foods into my repertoire, I became a less frazzled cook. I spent more time talking to the family and less time stirring the pot. It was a welcome change.

Convenience foods have become an integral part of my culinary style because they work for me, delivering speed, taste, and wholesomeness. I don't use convenience products all the time. There are occasions when I enjoy nothing more than chopping vegetables or browning beef for a stew. And I know nothing beats my homemade chocolate frosting, made with unsalted butter and the best-quality cocoa.

The purpose of *Cooking Out of the Box* is to show you how to make mealtime easier using convenience products in your cooking. You may choose to rely on boxed foods for all your meals or just when you're rushed. Never feel guilty that you're shortchanging your family if you don't scrape your knuckles grating potatoes for potato pancakes. Trust me, if you serve Extreme-Chocolate Cream Cheese Brownies, no one's going to ask whether the outrageous bars started with a brownie mix.

But don't be intimidated by boxed food, either. Boxes are culinary tools, just as flour and eggs or raw vegetables and meats are. Just because the directions on a package of soup mix say to "add water" doesn't mean you can't add chicken broth. Just because you're reconstituting instant vegetable soup doesn't mean you can't enhance it. Add a package of frozen vegetables and a cup of grated cheese and create an entrée from humble beginnings.

Although the title of the book is *Cooking Out of the Box,* the recipes will have you cooking out of packages, cans, containers, and jars as well. It's all in the spirit of convenience.

In some cases you may not find the product in the weight the recipe calls for. Manufacturers frequently change product size. No sweat. These recipes are flexible. Go up or down a couple of ounces, and your dish will still be great.

What's in the Cupboard?

While developing recipes for my family and for this book, I discovered some products that have become family favorites. I prize them for their flavor and their versatility. I'm not going to name brands because many companies put out similar products. Also, I don't want to be rigid about what products you need to buy. If you can't find, say, a package of navy bean soup to make this book's Navy Bean Kielbasa Soup, choose black bean soup. Your dish will taste different from the one in the book but equally good. As a general rule, I'd suggest buying products with the fewest seasonings added so that you have more flexibility.

That said, here are some products that surprised me with their versatility. I'd include them if I were helping you stock your cupboard. I also have suggestions for making box ingredients taste as good as fresh. Follow these tips, and you'll be thrilled to be cooking "out of the box."

1. Chocolate bars (Not as an instant meal, tempting though it may be, but as a flavoring, frosting, or chocolate boost.)
   - Break off a few squares of bittersweet chocolate, stir into a mug of hot milk, and you've got hot chocolate.
   - Place a piece of milk chocolate on top of a hot-from-the-oven chocolate chip cookie. Spread with a knife as the chocolate melts to glaze the cookie.

- Add a few squares of bittersweet chocolate to hot chocolate pudding to intensify the flavor.
2. Chocolate cookie crumbs (If you notice a theme here, it's that you can make any dessert taste better with chocolate.)
   - Stir together cookie crumbs and melted butter and use as a crust for a pie, cookie bars, or ice cream confections.
   - Layer cookie crumbs and vanilla pudding or vanilla yogurt for a yummy parfait.
   - Sprinkle cookie crumbs over light-colored ice cream, custard, or puddings.
3. Croutons
   - Coarsely crumble and use as a batter for fish or chicken.
   - Combine with eggs and cook as croquettes.
   - Mix with sausage for a casserole.
4. Dehydrated soup mixes
   - Use as a coating for baked chicken.
   - Reconstitute with half the liquid and use as a sauce.
   - Add sour cream and mayonnaise and have party dip.
5. Dehydrated hash brown potatoes
   - Combine with eggs and cook as potato pancakes.
   - Layer with chicken or sausage and cheese for a robust casserole.
6. Mashed potatoes
   - Add a cup of mashed potatoes to a cream soup as a thickener.
   - Stir a half cup of mashed potatoes into a bread machine bread batter. Your bread will be lighter and more tender.
   - Stir a half cup of mashed potatoes into a four- to six-egg omelet and turn it into a Spanish frittata.
7. Vegetables for stir-fry (I'm referring to fresh, sliced, and pared vegetables sold in plastic bags in produce sections.)
   - Cook vegetables in their package in a microwave oven. Mix with stir-fried beef or chicken. You'll cook a stir-fry meal in half the time with half the fat.

- Start with a dehydrated cream of vegetable soup, add the bag of vegetables, and savor a soup so chockful of nutrients your mom would be proud.
- Microwave a bag of vegetables, top with condensed cheese soup, and run the dish under the broiler—vegetables au gratin anyone?

Important Note

As I mentioned previously, manufacturers frequently call for you—the cook—to add ingredients to packaged mixes, such as eggs and oil for cakes or butter or margarine for mashed potatoes.

When using the "out of the box" recipes, read the instructions before cooking. Some recipes in this book tell you to follow package directions, but for most dishes, I added the package preparation ingredients in the recipes.

THE PATH TO PACKAGE PERFECTION— 10 TIPS TO ADD INSTANT FLAVOR TO BOXED FOODS:

1. Add a vegetable to an entrée recipe. Chopped red or green peppers, shredded carrots, or red cabbage, for example, add not only color and fresh taste but also crisp texture, vitamins, and fiber.
2. Just before you finish cooking a soup or stew, squirt in a little fresh lemon juice. The acid brings out the taste of the other seasonings.
3. Get your hand off the salt shaker. If packaged foods have one flaw, it's their high sodium content. Don't add salt to a dish until you've tasted it.
4. Vary condiments, and you'll vary flavors without any extra work. Instead of using red wine vinegar for all your dressings, try mellow balsamic vinegar or raspberry vinegar. Use garlic-flavored ketchup in a meatloaf or teriyaki sauce in place of steak sauce.

5. Turn a thin soup into a thick and hearty one. Remove some of the solids (meat or vegetables), puree in a blender, and return to the pot.
6. Add dry herbs for dishes that will cook at least 30 minutes. Add fresh herbs during the last 5 minutes of cooking. When substituting fresh for dry herbs, use two to three times the amount. Start with the smaller measure and add more according to your taste.
7. In cake, brownie, and cookie mixes that use margarine, substitute butter. It makes a remarkably delicious difference. You'll find that you can switch to melted butter in place of vegetable oil in many cake mixes as well.
8. If a casserole is completely cooked but still anemic looking, run the dish under the broiler for 30 seconds to 1 minute to brown.
9. Sprinkle casseroles with minced parsley, chives, or slivered almonds for eye and taste appeal.
10. Substitute scallions for onions. Not only are the green stalks easier to chop, but scallions will add welcome color to many soups, stews, or casseroles. Treat scallions like fresh herbs and add during the last 5 minutes of cooking.

appetizers and snacks

appetizers

Mushroom Tartlets

When baked, tartlet shells are light and crisp as any you would make from scratch.

MAKES 12 TARTLETS.

1	box frozen phyllo tartlet shells, thawed
1	tablespoon butter
1	cup coarsely chopped oyster, shiitake, or brown mushrooms
2	tablespoons minced shallot or onion
8	ounces shredded Swiss cheese
2	eggs
3/4	cup half-and-half
1/4	teaspoon ground pepper
1/2	teaspoon salt

Preheat oven to 325 degrees F.

Place tartlet shells on cookie sheet. Set aside.

Melt butter in small skillet. Add mushrooms and shallot and sauté over medium heat until mushrooms are tender and mixture is dry, about 5 minutes.

Spoon mushrooms into a bowl. Add cheese, eggs, and half-and-half. Beat with electric mixer. Stir in pepper and salt. Spoon mushroom mixture into tartlet shells.

Bake for 15 to 20 minutes or until knife inserted near center comes out clean. Allow tartlets to cool 5 minutes, then remove and serve.

Black Bean Cakes with Mango Salsa

Serve these as a first course to a sit-down dinner or place on a buffet table with the salsa accompaniment.

MAKES 24 TO 30 BEAN CAKES.

1	box (7 ounces) seasoned black beans
1	egg, beaten
1/4	cup chopped onion, shallot, or scallion
1/4	cup vegetable oil
1	jar (12 to 16 ounces) mango salsa

Bring 2 cups water to boil in 3-quart pot. Add beans and stir. Cover pot. Remove from heat and set aside 5 minutes until very thick. Stir in egg and onion.

Heat 2 tablespoons of the oil in 12-inch nonstick skillet. Drop in bean mixture by the rounded tablespoon. Flatten to 1/2-inch thickness. Fry over medium heat 3 minutes on first side and 2 to 3 minutes on second side or until firm and lightly browned. Remove and keep warm. Repeat with remaining bean mixture, adding oil as needed.

Arrange bean cakes on a platter and spoon mango salsa into a bowl in the center.

Barbecued Chicken Crescents with Dipping Sauce

Look for cooked, shredded barbecued chicken in the deli or the refrigerated, prepared meat counter of your supermarket.

MAKES 32 CRESCENTS.

4	cans (11.3 ounces each) refrigerated dinner roll dough*
1	container (32 ounces) barbecued, shredded chicken
1 1/2	cups bottled sweet and sour sauce

Preheat oven to 375 degrees F.

Working with one roll at a time, press or roll into a 5-inch circle. Place 2 tablespoons shredded chicken in center of each. Fold in half and press edges with tines of fork to seal.

Place on greased cookie sheet. Bake 10 to 13 minutes or until golden. Serve with sweet and sour sauce for dipping.

Variation: Use barbecued pork instead of chicken.

*Each can yields 8 rolls. If buying larger cans, your total should be 32.

Tomato Bruschetta

Make this appetizer during the summer when you have juicy, sweet tomatoes as a topping.

SERVES 8.

1	box (8 slices) frozen Texas garlic toast
4	tomatoes, thinly sliced
1	teaspoon crushed, dried oregano

Preheat oven to 425 degrees F.

Arrange garlic toast on cookie sheet. Bake for 4 to 5 minutes.

Arrange tomato slices over toast. Sprinkle each slice with ⅛ teaspoon oregano. Return to oven and bake another 3 to 5 minutes or until tomatoes are hot. Remove from oven and serve immediately.

ADD A TOUCH:
Top each serving with 1 tablespoon grated Parmesan when you sprinkle on oregano.

Onion-Topped Chile Con Queso

To keep this dip hot throughout a party, spoon into a fondue pot and place over canned heat.

SERVES 10.

1	box (1 pound) processed American cheese, cut in cubes
1	can (14 ounces) diced tomatoes with green chiles
1	can (3.5 ounces) fried onions
	Tortilla chips

ADD A TOUCH:

Serve with
cauliflower and
broccoli florets.

Combine cheese and tomatoes in heavy-bottomed pot. Cook over low heat, stirring frequently until cheese melts.

Pour into shallow serving bowl. Sprinkle with fried onions. Serve with tortilla chips.

appetizers and snacks

Hot Bean Dip

Bean mixes are ideal in dips. The beans are flavored and finely chopped, which means you have to do less preparation.

SERVES 6.

1 3/4	cups boiling water
1	box (7 ounces) refried bean mix
1	cup grated Mexican cheese
3/4	cup salsa
3/4	cup sour cream
	Tortilla chips

Preheat oven to 350 degrees F.

In a medium bowl, combine boiling water and refried bean mix. Stir well. Cover and let sit 5 minutes.

Spoon beans into ovenproof casserole dish. Top with cheese. Bake 10 minutes or until cheese is melted and mixture is hot.

Remove from oven. Spread on salsa, then add dollops of sour cream. Serve with tortilla chips.

Baked Vegetable Spread

If you're counting calories, substitute light cream cheese and light mayonnaise in this recipe. It will be just as smooth-textured and delicious.

SERVES 10.

2	packages (8 ounces each) cream cheese
1	cup mayonnaise
1	package (1.68 ounces) home-style vegetable soup and dip mix
1	package (10 ounces) frozen, chopped spinach, thawed and drained
	Crackers

Preheat oven to 350 degrees F.

In bowl of electric mixer, combine cream cheese, mayonnaise, vegetable soup mix, and spinach. Beat until blended.

Spoon mixture into shallow casserole dish with 9- to 10-inch diameter. Bake 25 minutes or until mixture is hot and lightly browned. Serve with crackers.

Cheese Torta

You'll find layered cheese and pesto "cakes" in all the best gourmet shops, but you can make the same dish at home for a fraction of the cost.

SERVES 12.

1	package (8 ounces) and 1 package (3 ounces) plain cream cheese
3	tablespoons sun-dried tomato pesto
3	tablespoons basil pesto
	Thinly sliced French bread

In bowl of electric mixer, beat cream cheese until fluffy.

Line a 3-by-5-inch loaf pan with plastic wrap.

Spread one-third cream cheese in bottom of pan. Top with tomato pesto. Add second layer of cheese. Top with basil pesto. Add remaining cheese, spreading in even layer. Press down with back of spoon to create firm loaf.

Wrap in plastic wrap and chill 3 hours or overnight.

To serve, turn loaf out onto serving platter. Arrange bread slices on the side.

ADD A TOUCH:
Decorate the top of the loaf with fresh basil leaves or sprinkle with pine nuts.

Scallion-Artichoke Dip

Blend cream cheese with scallions for a pastel green dip. Accent the color by spooning the mixture into a serving "bowl" made from a hollowed-out artichoke, green cabbage, or bell pepper.

MAKES ABOUT 2 CUPS.

1	package (8 ounces) cream cheese
2	teaspoons lemon juice
2	tablespoons milk or half-and-half
3	scallions, ends trimmed, coarsely chopped
1	can (8.5 ounces) artichoke hearts, well drained
	Crackers or sliced cocktail rye bread

In blender or food processor, combine cream cheese, lemon juice, milk, and scallions. Blend well. Mixture will turn pastel green.

Add artichoke hearts and process for 30 seconds or just long enough to mince artichokes. Spoon out into serving bowl and serve with crackers or bread.

appetizers and snacks

Smoked Salmon Quesadillas

The crisp outer tortilla shell and the smooth cream cheese filling make these appetizers a marvelous morsel.

SERVES 12.

1	package (8 ounces) smoked-salmon-flavored cream cheese
6	(8-inch) flour tortillas
3	tablespoons butter

Divide cream cheese among tortillas, spreading on one half of each tortilla. Fold tortillas in half.

Melt 1 tablespoon butter in 10-inch skillet. Add two folded tortillas. Sauté over medium heat 2 to 3 minutes per side or until golden brown. Remove and keep warm. Repeat with remaining tortillas, adding more butter as needed.

Cut each folded tortilla in half to form quarters and serve.

ADD A TOUCH:
Before sautéing, arrange a thin slice of fresh tomato over cream cheese.

snacks

Cheese Poppers

If you like Cheddar cheese crackers, you'll love this spicy home-baked version. Poppers will keep in a covered container in the freezer for a couple of months.

MAKES 3¹/₂ TO 4 DOZEN POPPERS.

1	tablespoon unsalted butter
4	ounces grated Cheddar cheese
1	teaspoon hot red pepper sauce
1¹/₃	cups piecrust mix

ADD A TOUCH:
Blend ¹/₂ cup finely chopped pecans into batter.

Preheat oven to 375 degrees F.

In bowl of electric mixer, beat together butter, cheese, and red pepper sauce until fluffy. Blend in piecrust mix. Add a few drops of water (if necessary) for dough to come together.

Shape into balls using 1 heaping teaspoon dough per popper. Place on ungreased cookie sheet. Flatten slightly with finger to create disk about ¹/₃ inch high and 1 inch in diameter. Bake 13 minutes or until lightly browned.

Remove from oven; cool on wire rack and serve.

Wonton Crisps

These crunchy, savory wonton snacks taste best when hot from the oven. Use other cheeses, such as Asiago or Cheddar, if you prefer.

MAKES 36 CRISPS.

1	package (about 1 pound) refrigerated wonton skins
1	egg, beaten with 1 tablespoon water
3/4	cup grated Parmesan cheese
1	teaspoon crushed, dried oregano

Preheat oven to 400 degrees F.

Remove 36 wonton skins and arrange on cookie sheet. Brush with egg.

In a bowl, mix together cheese and oregano. Sprinkle 1 teaspoon cheese mixture over each wonton. Bake for 3 to 5 minutes or until cheese melts and wontons are crisp. Remove from cookie sheet and serve immediately.

ADD A TOUCH:

Add a few drops of hot red pepper sauce to egg before brushing wonton skins.

Sweet and Salty Nibbles

"Gourmet" snack mixes with chunks of chocolate, dried fruit, and nuts are easy to make at home using your favorite crisp and crunchy cereal.

MAKES 20 NIBBLES.

1¹/₂	cups dry-roasted, unsalted almonds
1¹/₂	cups salted cashews
1	cup dried cranberries
1	cup square oat cereal
¹/₄	cup semisweet or bittersweet chocolate chips

On a cookie sheet combine nuts, cranberries, and cereal.

Place semisweet chocolate in microwave-safe dish and microwave at medium heat 2 minutes. Drizzle over nuts and cereal.

Toss lightly. Chill in refrigerator 3 hours or until firm. Break into small chunks. Serve immediately or store in airtight container for up to 1 week.

Pecan-Caramel-Cinnamon Crunch

Butter, caramel, and pecans raise cereal snacks to new taste levels.

MAKES 8 CUPS.

6	cups cinnamon crunch cereal squares
2	cups chopped pecans
3/4	cup good-quality caramel sauce
1/4	teaspoon salt
1	tablespoon butter

Preheat oven to 325 degrees F.

Stir cereal and pecans together in large bowl.

In a small, microwave-safe bowl, combine caramel sauce, salt, and butter. Microwave on high heat 1 minute or until butter melts and caramel sauce thins slightly. Pour over cereal mixture. Stir gently but well.

Line a cookie sheet with wax paper. Pour cereal mixture onto cookie sheet. Bake for 10 minutes. Remove from oven, stir, and return for another 5 to 8 minutes or until nuts are golden brown and mixture is fragrant.

Immediately remove from oven. Mixture will be soft but will firm up as it cools. When mixture is room temperature, break into bite-size pieces. Serve immediately or store in airtight container for up to one week.

Hot Bites

This spicy snack registers mild on the heat scale. If you want to add a few sparks, sprinkle on hot red pepper sauce.

MAKES 10 CUPS.

1/3	cup margarine or butter
1	envelope (1.25 ounces) mild taco seasoning mix
6	cups corn squares cereal
2	cups raw almonds, peanuts, or pecans
2	cups pretzel nuggets, preferably unsalted

Preheat oven to 300 degrees F.

Melt margarine in a large pot. Stir in taco seasoning mix, cereal, nuts, and pretzels. Spread in shallow roasting pan. Bake for 30 minutes, stirring every 10 minutes. Remove from oven and cool before serving.

soups for starters or the whole meal

Corn Chowder

The smoky flavor of ham enhances a convenience package of cream of corn soup. The taste is even better if you make this soup in advance and reheat it.

SERVES 4.

1	box (16 ounces) cream of corn soup or corn chowder
1	cup diced ham
1	cup half-and-half

In 3-quart pot combine all ingredients. Simmer 5 minutes to heat through. Remove from heat and serve.

Egg-Lemon Soup with Chicken

NOTE:

In your local gro-
cery store, a few
steps away from
the raw meat and
poultry, you'll now
find—in boxes—
precooked ground
beef, barbecued
shredded pork,
grilled baby back
ribs, hamburger
patties, chicken,
and even pot roasts
and stews. Just
open a package,
heat it up in the
microwave or throw
it in a pan with
other ingredients,
and it's ready to go!

*Combining eggs and lemon juice is a
trick used by Greek cooks to thicken
and flavor soups and sauces.*

SERVES 4.

1   packet from 5-ounce box chicken
        noodle soup mix
1   egg
2   tablespoons fresh lemon juice
1   box (6 ounces) plain, roasted, sliced
        chicken breast

Bring 1 quart water to boil in 3-quart
pot. Add soup packet. Cook over
medium heat 5 minutes.

In bowl, beat egg until foamy. Slowly
beat in lemon juice. Gradually beat 1 cup
hot soup into egg mixture.

Pour egg mixture into soup pot. Add
chicken and heat through. Do not boil,
or egg will curdle. Remove from heat
and serve.

Hot and Sour Soup

The combination of citrus juice and crushed red pepper flakes makes this soup a delicious alternative to penicillin for a cold.

SERVES 4.

1	box (1 quart) chicken broth
1	tablespoon lime juice
1/4	cup finely chopped scallion
1/4	teaspoon crushed red pepper flakes
1	cup garlic croutons

Pour chicken broth into 3-quart pot. Bring to a boil. Add lime juice, scallion, crushed red pepper flakes, and croutons. Stir well.

Cover pot. Remove from heat and let stand 5 minutes. Serve immediately.

ADD A TOUCH: Stir in 1 cup diced cooked chicken and sprinkle with 2 tablespoons minced cilantro before serving.

Tomato-Basil Soup

Double the tomato flavor by adding tomato paste to a packaged tomato soup. Fresh basil is a favorite herbal accent.

SERVES 4.

1	tablespoon olive oil
1/2	cup minced onion
2	tablespoons tomato paste
1	box (1 quart) creamy tomato soup
1/4	cup fresh minced basil

ADD A TOUCH:

Fry 4 strips bacon, crumble, and sprinkle into the soup just before serving.

Heat oil in 3-quart pot. Add onion and sauté 5 minutes. Add tomato paste and tomato soup. Simmer 5 minutes or until hot.

Pour soup into 4 bowls; top each serving with 1 tablespoon basil and serve.

French Onion Soup

Top onion soup with a layer of bread and cheese, but don't make the topping too thick, or it will be heavy and soggy, not crisp.

SERVES 4.

1	tablespoon olive oil
2	small onions, cut into $1/4$-inch-thick slices
1	box (1 quart) onion soup
4	($1/2$-inch-thick) slices slightly stale French bread
1	cup grated Gruyère cheese

Heat oil in large nonstick pot. Add onions and cook over low heat until tender, but not browned, about 10 minutes. Add soup. Bring to a boil.

Ladle soup into 4 large soup bowls.

Top each bowl with a slice of bread. Sprinkle $1/4$ cup cheese over each bread slice and serve.

Vichyssoise

Keep this soup in a pitcher in the refrigerator for instant summer lunches. It will keep up to four days.

SERVES 6.

3	cups milk
1	package (11 ounces) creamy potato soup mix
1	cup finely chopped scallions
2	cups sour cream

ADD A TOUCH:

Add 2 cups chopped, cooked crabmeat or shrimp and 1 tablespoon minced fresh parsley just before serving.

Pour milk into 5-quart pot. Add 4 cups water and bring to a simmer. Whisk in potato soup mix. Cook over medium heat, stirring frequently, until thick, about 10 minutes. Remove from heat.

Stir in scallions and sour cream. Chill and serve.

Apple-Squash Spice Soup

Natural food stores and many supermarkets carry boxes of soy-based vegetarian soup. Add a few aromatic spices to refresh the flavor.

SERVES 4.

1	tablespoon butter or vegetable oil
1	large apple, peeled and minced
3/4	teaspoon cinnamon
1	box (1 quart) butternut or pumpkin soup
	Salt and pepper to taste

Melt butter or pour vegetable oil in 3-quart pot. Add apple and sauté 5 minutes. Stir in cinnamon. Cook 30 seconds. Stir in soup. Simmer 5 minutes or until hot.

    Season with salt and pepper to taste.

ADD A TOUCH:
Top each serving with 1 tablespoon sour cream or unsweetened whipped cream.

Minted Pea Soup

If you hate peas, substitute a pound of frozen, sliced carrots for an equally satisfying and delicious dish.

SERVES 4.

1	bag (1 pound) frozen baby peas, unthawed
1	can (14 to 16 ounces) chicken broth
1/4	cup whipping cream
1/2	teaspoon salt
1/2	teaspoon pepper
3	tablespoons fresh minced mint leaves

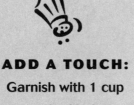

ADD A TOUCH:
Garnish with 1 cup cooked baby shrimp.

In a small pot, combine peas and chicken broth and simmer 10 minutes or until peas are tender and mixture is hot.

Stir in cream, salt, pepper, and mint. Simmer 2 minutes or until hot.

Remove to blender and puree. Serve hot.

Cold Cucumber Soup

Make a pitcher of cucumber soup in the morning and refrigerate. You'll have a refreshing first course waiting for dinner.

SERVES 4.

1	medium cucumber, peeled and cut into large chunks
1	tablespoon dill sprigs
2	scallions, trimmed, or ¼ cup chopped onion
1	quart buttermilk
	Salt and pepper to taste

In a blender, combine cucumber, dill, scallions or onion, and buttermilk. Blend until vegetables are minced.

Spoon mixture into serving bowl or pitcher. Add salt and pepper to taste. Let stand 5 minutes before serving.

hearty soups

Black Bean Chorizo Soup

Chorizo, a finely ground Mexican pork sausage, is so well seasoned that you don't have to add a lot of spices to this dish. If you can't find it, substitute hot Italian sausage.

SERVES 4.

8	ounces chorizo
1	box (7 ounces) black bean mix
1	can (1 quart) chicken broth
1 1/2	tablespoons fresh lime juice
	Freshly ground pepper to taste

ADD A TOUCH:
Top each serving with 1 tablespoon each chopped red onions, minced cilantro, and sour cream.

In large pot, brown chorizo and break up with back of spoon. Pour off any fat.

Stir in bean mix and chicken broth. Bring to a boil. Reduce heat to low. Cover and simmer 5 minutes.

Stir in lime juice and pepper to taste.

To serve, ladle soup into bowls.

soups for starters or the whole meal

Minestrone

To give a canned or boxed soup a fresh, sprightly taste, add a dash of lemon juice just before serving.

SERVES 4.

2	cans (14 to 16 ounces each) chicken broth
1	box (6.5 ounces) country French beans with gemelli
2	cans (14 ounces each) zucchini with Italian style tomatoes
1/4	cup minced fresh basil
1	tablespoon fresh lemon juice

Bring chicken broth to a boil in 5-quart pot. Add beans. Stir and return to boil. Cover. Reduce heat and simmer 15 minutes.

Stir in zucchini and basil. Simmer 2 minutes to heat through. Stir in lemon juice, remove from heat, and serve.

Navy Bean Kielbasa Soup

If you add vegetables and meat, soup cups are filling enough to serve as an entrée.

SERVES 4 AS AN ENTRÉE.

1	bag (1 pound) frozen mixed potatoes, carrots, and onions
1/2	teaspoon salt
	Nonstick cooking spray
1	package (12 ounces) turkey or fat-reduced kielbasa, cut into 1/2-inch-thick slices
3	soup cup packages (about 1 cup each) navy bean soup
1	can (1 quart) chicken broth
1/4	teaspoon pepper

In a medium pot, combine frozen vegetables and salt. Add 1 cup water. Bring to a boil and cook at medium heat until vegetables are tender, about 5 minutes. Drain.

Meanwhile, spray medium pot with cooking spray. Add kielbasa slices. Sauté over medium heat 5 minutes, stirring frequently until meat is slightly browned.

Add soup mix, chicken broth, pepper, and cooked vegetables to kielbasa. Stir well. Bring to a boil. Cover, reduce heat to low, and simmer 5 minutes or until soup is slightly thickened. Serve while hot.

soups for starters or the whole meal

Cheesy Chowder

Cheese soup, a sublime comfort food, is also a good source of calcium—a mineral your whole family needs.

SERVES 4 TO 6 AS AN ENTRÉE.

1	tablespoon butter
1	box (9 ounces) frozen mixed vegetables
1	tablespoon flour
1	box (4.5 ounces) julienne potato with cheese mix
5	cups milk, divided
1	cup shredded Cheddar cheese
1/4	teaspoon salt
1/4	teaspoon pepper

In large pot, melt butter. Add frozen vegetables and sauté 5 minutes. Stir in flour to make a thick mixture. Stir in potato and cheese mix. Add 2 cups milk and cook over medium heat, stirring constantly until very thick. Reduce heat to low.

Stir in cheese, 1/2 cup at a time, and allow to melt in. Add remaining milk. Stir well. Simmer until potatoes are tender and soup is thick, about 15 minutes. Add salt and pepper and serve while hot.

Cajun Chicken Soup

Instead of choosing between chicken and sausage, Louisiana cooks often use both for texture and flavor.

SERVES 4.

1	tablespoon vegetable oil
1/2	cup diced green bell pepper
1/2	cup diced onion
1/2	cup diced pepperoni
1	box (6 ounces) roasted, sliced chicken breast
1	box (5.7 ounces) Cajun-style rice and pasta mix

Heat oil in 3-quart pot. Add bell pepper and onion and sauté 10 minutes over low heat. Stir in pepperoni and chicken. Add rice and pasta mix.

Add 2¼ cups water. Bring to a boil over medium heat, uncovered, for 10 minutes, stirring occasionally or until rice is tender. Remove from heat and serve while hot.

Hot and Spicy Roast Chicken and Rice Soup

When you're cutting up a chile for this recipe, wash your hands well before you touch your eyes. A chile's volatile oils are very irritating.

SERVES 4.

1	tablespoon vegetable oil
1	serrano or jalapeño chile, cored, seeded, and minced
2	cans (14 to 16 ounces each) chicken broth
1	can (14 ounces) diced tomatoes
1	cup instant rice
1	box (10 ounces) roasted, sliced chicken breast
1/4	teaspoon salt
1/4	teaspoon pepper

Heat oil in medium pot. Add chile and sauté 3 minutes. Add broth and tomatoes with liquid. Bring to a boil. Add rice. Stir. Cover and remove from heat. Let stand 5 minutes.

Cut or tear chicken into bite-size pieces. Add to soup. Stir in salt and pepper. Simmer 3 to 5 minutes or until hot. Remove from heat and serve.

ADD A TOUCH: Sprinkle each serving with 1 tablespoon minced cilantro and 1/4 cup coarsely crushed tortilla chips.

Chicken-Spinach Chowder

Keep the heat low when you're cooking a milk-based soup. Boiling may cause the milk to curdle.

SERVES 6.

6	cups milk, divided
1	box (10 ounces) chicken noodle soup mix
1	package (10 ounces) frozen, chopped spinach
1	box (10 ounces) roasted, sliced chicken breast

Heat 1 cup milk in 3-quart pot. Add entire box of noodle soup mix, remaining 5 cups milk, spinach, and chicken. Cook over low heat 10 minutes or until hot. Remove from heat and serve.

Ramen Noodle-Shrimp Soup

Packets of Ramen noodles make a convenient snack, but for a meal you'll want to add vegetables and seafood or chicken.

SERVES 4.

2   packages (3.5 ounces each) shrimp-flavored Ramen
      noodles
1   package (10 ounces) frozen, chopped vegetables
2   cups diced, cooked shrimp

Bring 4 cups water to boil in a 3-quart pot. Add both packages noodles and vegetables. Cook at low boil 3 minutes or until noodles are tender. Stir in shrimp and heat through. Remove from heat and serve.

Curried Shrimp Noodle Soup

Your kitchen is a lot more convenient than carryout when you crave a Thai dinner. Start with a noodle soup kit and add fresh vegetables and seafood for an entrée in a bowl.

SERVES 4.

1	box (5.7 ounces) Thai rice noodle soup
1	tablespoon vegetable oil
1	package (1 pound) frozen mixed vegetables
1/2	teaspoon crushed red pepper flakes
1 1/4	cups chicken broth
1/2	cup milk
1	package (12 ounces) frozen cooked, peeled shrimp
1/4	cup chopped cilantro
1	tablespoon lime juice

Bring 3 cups water to boil in 3-quart pot. Add noodles. Simmer 2 to 3 minutes or until tender. Drain and reserve.

Heat oil in 5-quart pot. Add mixed vegetables and sauté 5 minutes or until limp. Add red pepper flakes and seasoning packet from the noodle soup. Stir in broth and milk. Bring to a boil.

Reduce heat to low. Stir in shrimp. Cook soup on low heat 2 minutes to thaw shrimp. Add noodles, cilantro, and lime juice. Simmer 1 minute. Remove from heat and serve.

Tortellini Asparagus Soup

Use your favorite green vegetable, such as green beans, sugar snap peas, or snow peas, to add color and nutrients to this simple soup.

SERVES 4.

1	box (8.9 ounces) dried cheese or meat tortellini
1/2	pound fresh asparagus, tough ends removed, cut into 1-inch lengths
6	cups chicken broth
1/4	cup minced scallions

Place tortellini in 3-quart pot. Add asparagus and broth and bring to a boil.

Reduce heat to medium and simmer 10 minutes or until tortellini are tender. Remove from heat, sprinkle with scallions, and serve.

Sherried Mushroom and Wild Rice Soup

This soup makes an elegant vegetarian entrée. Round out the meal with Southwestern Cheddar Scones (see page 170).

SERVES 4.

2	tablespoons butter
1/4	cup minced onion
1	can (14 ounces) cream of mushroom soup
2	cans (14 to 16 ounces each) vegetable broth
1	box (2.75 ounces) quick-cooking wild rice
1/4	cup heavy cream
1/2	teaspoon salt
1/4	teaspoon pepper

In medium pot, melt butter. Add onion. Sauté 5 minutes over medium heat or until tender. Stir in mushroom soup and broth. Add wild rice.

Cover and cook 5 minutes over medium heat. Reduce heat to low. Stir in cream, salt, and pepper. Cook 1 minute, remove from heat, and serve.

simple and savory entrées

Mediterranean Roast Chicken

Salad dressing bathes chicken in marinating flavors so you can skip the extra seasonings.

SERVES 4.

2/3   cup bottled Italian salad dressing
3   pounds chicken, cut into pieces

Pour salad dressing into large bowl. Add chicken pieces to dressing, turn to coat well. Cover and refrigerate 4 to 5 hours.

Preheat oven to 400 degrees F.

Remove chicken from dressing marinade. Place on cookie sheet and baste with marinade. Bake 40 minutes or until thoroughly cooked and browned. Remove from oven and serve.

Hot-Sweet Baked Chicken

Choose a brand of orange marmalade that isn't too sweet to use as a basting or barbecue sauce.

SERVES 4.

3	pounds chicken, cut into pieces
	Olive-oil flavored cooking spray
1/2	cup barbecue sauce
2	tablespoons orange marmalade
1	tablespoon butter

ADD A TOUCH:
Sprinkle chicken with chopped parsley and serve with rice on the side.

Preheat oven to 350 degrees F.

Place chicken pieces in shallow roasting pan. Spray with cooking spray and bake for 30 minutes.

In a small pan, stir together barbecue sauce and marmalade. Bring to a boil. Remove from heat and add butter. Remove chicken from oven, baste generously, and return to oven another 30 minutes. Remove from oven and serve.

Meatloaf with Mashed Potato Crust

Bake mashed potatoes on top of meatloaf to keep the meat moist. Potato lovers can double the recipe and serve extra mashed potatoes on the side.

SERVES 4.

1	can (14.5 ounces) diced tomatoes with green chiles, drained
1	pound ground chuck
1	slice firm white bread, torn into small pieces
1/4	cup chopped onion
1	egg, beaten
1/2	teaspoon salt
1/2	teaspoon pepper
1	box (7.6 ounces) sour cream and chive mashed potato mix

Preheat oven to 350 degrees F.

In a bowl, combine canned tomatoes, beef, bread, onion, egg, salt, and pepper. Spoon meat mixture into 9-by-5-inch loaf pan.

Prepare mashed potatoes according to package directions.

Spread mashed potatoes over meatloaf and completely cover. Bake 1 hour or until golden brown. Remove from oven and serve.

Grilled Asian Flank Steak

For warm-weather dining, marinate flank steak in the morning, then grill the meat outdoors instead of broiling it for dinner.

SERVES 4.

1	tablespoon soy sauce
$2/3$	cup balsamic vinaigrette dressing
1	pound flank steak

In a large bowl, stir together soy sauce and dressing.

Make shallow diagonal slashes on both sides of steak. Add meat to dressing mixture and marinate in refrigerator 4 to 6 hours.

Place meat on broiler pan. Broil 6 minutes each side for medium doneness. Remove from broiler. Cut meat into thin slices against the grain and serve.

Variation: Serve the meat in flour tortillas for a wrap. Add strips of roasted red pepper.

simple and savory entrées

Cornbread-Coated Perch

Gently crush seasoned stuffing mix and use as a crunchy coating to skillet-cooked fish. Use cornbread or experiment with other bread stuffings.

SERVES 4.

1	tablespoon butter
1	celery stalk, trimmed and diced, about $1/2$ cup
3	ounces cornbread stuffing mix
	Grated rind of 1 lemon
1	egg
4	large or 8 small perch fillets
1	tablespoon vegetable oil
4	lemon wedges

Melt butter in large skillet. Add celery and sauté 5 minutes or until tender. Remove celery but leave any butter in skillet.

On a dinner plate, combine celery, stuffing mix, and lemon rind. Stir to mix.

Beat egg in a bowl. Dip each perch fillet in egg, then roll in stuffing mix to coat on all sides.

Add oil to butter in skillet. Heat over medium heat 30 seconds. Arrange perch in skillet. Sauté 5 minutes per side or until stuffing is golden brown and fish is cooked through to the center.

Remove fish to a serving plate and garnish with lemon wedges.

ADD A TOUCH: Heat up any left-over stuffing mix, toss with about $1/4$ cup chicken broth, and serve on the side.

Sweet and Hot Baby Back Ribs

Barbecue sauces, such as this one with a high sugar content, should be added to ribs toward the end of cooking to avoid burning.

SERVES 4.

4	packages (1 pound each) precooked pork loin ribs
1	cup smoky barbecue sauce
1/4	cup orange marmalade
1/4	cup chili sauce

Preheat oven to 350 degrees F.

Cover a large, shallow roasting pan with foil. Add ribs and bake for 10 minutes.

Stir together barbecue sauce, marmalade, and chili sauce in a bowl. Remove ribs from oven, slather with sauce, and bake another 10 minutes, or until heated through. Remove from oven and serve.

Pork Tenderloin with Chutney

Fruit chutneys are wonderful for adding moisture to lean pork cuts.

SERVES 4.

1	pork tenderloin (1 pound)
1/4	teaspoon salt
1/4	teaspoon pepper
1	jar (about 10 ounces) fruit chutney of your choice

Preheat oven to 400 degrees F.

Place pork on rack over shallow roasting pan. Season with salt and pepper. Roast for 25 to 30 minutes or until meat thermometer registers 155 degrees.

Slice pork 1/4 inch thick and arrange on plates. Top with chutney.

ADD A TOUCH:
For an attractive presentation, arrange pork slices in a ring on a platter and garnish the plate with sliced ripe pears. Pass the chutney separately.

Salmon with Lemon–Leek Sauce

Delicate leek sauce, spiked with a dash of lemon juice, brings out the rich flavor of fresh salmon.

SERVES 4.

2	tablespoons butter
4	salmon fillets (6 ounces each)
	Salt and pepper to taste
	Lemon–Leek Sauce (follows)
4	lemon wedges

Melt butter in 12-inch skillet.

Season salmon fillets with salt and pepper. Add salmon to skillet in one layer. Cook over medium heat 5 minutes per side or until fish is cooked through.

Prepare Lemon–Leek Sauce.

Arrange fish fillets on 4 plates. Top each with some Lemon–Leek Sauce, and garnish each plate with a lemon wedge. Serve remaining Lemon–Leek Sauce on the side.

Lemon–Leek Sauce

1	box (1.8 ounces) leek soup dip and recipe mix
2	cups milk
1	tablespoon fresh lemon juice

In a small pot, combine leek soup and milk. Bring to a boil. Reduce heat to low. Stir and simmer 5 minutes or until mixture is thick. Stir in lemon juice.

simple and savory entrées

Chile-Beef Roast

Add a pound of small red potatoes and/or baby carrots to the roast and let the vegetables cook with the beef.

SERVES 6.

1	top round roast (2 pounds)
1	jar (12 ounces) chili sauce
1	tablespoon Dijon-style mustard
1	tablespoon white wine vinegar
1	tablespoon brown sugar

Preheat oven to 500 degrees F.

Place beef in shallow roasting pan. Roast for 15 minutes.

Meanwhile, combine chili sauce, mustard, vinegar, and brown sugar in a bowl. Stir well.

Remove meat from oven. Coat with chili mixture. Cover beef loosely with foil.

Reduce oven temperature to 325 degrees. Return beef to oven and roast 1 hour or until meat thermometer registers 135 degrees. Remove beef from oven and let roast stand 5 minutes to firm up. Thinly slice beef to serve.

Ginger-Glazed Pork over Cornbread Stuffing

Lean pork chops can be dry, but an apricot glaze keeps the meat moist and tender.

SERVES 4.

1	tablespoon vegetable oil
4	center-cut pork chops (4 ounces each)
3	cups cornbread stuffing mix
1	cup chicken broth
1/4	teaspoon ground ginger
1/4	cup apricot preserves

Preheat oven to 325 degrees F.

Heat oil in 10-inch ovenproof skillet. Add pork chops and brown 3 minutes per side over medium heat. Remove pork chops and set aside.

Add stuffing mix and chicken broth to skillet. Stir to moisten. Return pork chops to the skillet.

In a cup, stir together ginger and preserves. Spoon over pork chops. Bake for 20 minutes or until pork chops are cooked through. Remove from oven and serve.

Mustard-Herb Crusted Chicken

If you like crunchy chicken, you'll love what you taste when you make this recipe.

SERVES 4.

1/4	cup (1/2 stick) butter or margarine
1	tablespoon Dijon-style mustard
1	small chicken, cut into serving portions
2	cups crushed herb-seasoned stuffing mix

Preheat oven to 400 degrees F.

In a small pot, heat together butter and mustard. Coat chicken with butter mixture, reserving any leftover mixture. Place chicken in shallow roasting pan.

Generously coat chicken with stuffing mix, pressing in. Drizzle chicken with any remaining butter mixture. Bake for 45 minutes or until cooked through. Remove from oven and serve.

ADD A TOUCH:
Use homemade bread crumbs flavored with a pinch each of thyme and oregano.

meals-in-one: casseroles, skillet dinners, and stews

casseroles

Cheese Strata

SERVES 6.

To save last-minute preparation time, assemble this dish in advance and refrigerate up to 12 hours.

1   package (3.8 ounces) three-cheese and broccoli soup mix
          or Cheddar cheese soup mix

3   cups milk

1   package (8 ounces) shredded sharp Cheddar cheese

5   slices white bread

Preheat oven to 325 degrees F.

In a medium pot, combine soup mix and milk. Stir well and bring to a boil. Reduce heat to low and cook 5 minutes, stirring

ADD A TOUCH:
Steam 2 cups broc-
coli florets. Arrange
broccoli over
first layer of
cheese sauce.

frequently or until thick. Stir half the
cheese into the soup.

Cut bread slices in half.

Grease deep 9-inch square glass
baking dish. Arrange half the bread in
one layer in dish. Spoon half the cheese
sauce over the bread. Top with remaining bread. Spoon on remaining sauce.
Sprinkle with remaining cheese.

Bake 45 minutes or until strata is
puffed and golden. Remove from oven.
Let set 5 minutes before cutting and
serving.

Macaroni and Cheese Pizza Casserole

If your family can't decide between the comforts of macaroni and cheese or the spicy goodness of a pepperoni pizza, combine the two in a hearty casserole.

SERVES 6.

1	box (24 ounces) shells and cheese or macaroni and cheese
4	ounces sliced or diced pepperoni
1	can (14.5 ounces) diced tomatoes, drained
2	cups shredded mozzarella

Preheat oven to 350 degrees F.

Prepare shells and cheese according to package directions. Stir in pepperoni and tomatoes.

Spread mixture in greased 9-inch square glass baking dish. Top with shredded cheese. Bake 10 minutes or until cheese melts and is bubbly. Remove from oven and serve.

ADD A TOUCH:
Before baking, top casserole with 1 green bell pepper, cored, seeded, and sliced in rings.

Nacho Chili Enchiladas

Canned cheese soup with a spicier nacho cheese flavor doubles as a sauce in Southwestern dishes. If you're using regular cheese soup instead, add a generous dash of hot red pepper sauce.

SERVES 4.

1	box (10 ounces) cooked chicken breast
1	can (11 ounces) condensed nacho cheese soup, divided
1/4	cup sour cream, divided
3/4	cup grated Mexican cheese blend
4	(9-inch) flour tortillas

ADD A TOUCH:
Stir 2 tablespoons chives into the sour cream. Top with tomato salsa just before serving.

Preheat oven to 350 degrees F.

In a bowl, combine chicken, ½ cup nacho cheese soup, 2 tablespoons sour cream, and grated cheese.

Spoon mixture down center of tortillas, dividing evenly among tortillas. Roll up and place tortillas, seam side down, in greased 9-inch square baking dish. Stir together remaining soup and sour cream and spread over tortillas. Bake 20 minutes or until golden. Remove from heat and serve.

Chicken Pot Pie

Heat the mixture of chicken and vegetables before spooning it into a baking dish, and a pot pie will bake faster and more evenly.

SERVES 4.

1	refrigerated piecrust
1	box (10 ounces) roasted, sliced chicken breast
1	can (10.75 ounces) condensed cream of celery soup
3	cups frozen mixed corn, peppers, and onion

Preheat oven to 400 degrees F.

Unfold piecrust if folded, and set aside.

In a 3-quart pot, combine chicken, celery soup, and frozen mixed vegetables. Simmer 5 minutes to thaw vegetables.

Spoon chicken mixture into 9-inch pie plate. Arrange piecrust over chicken, trimming off any excess. Make 2 or 3 slashes in top of crust for steam to escape.

Bake for 20 minutes or until crust is golden brown and filling is bubbling. Remove from oven and serve.

Variation: Skip the piecrust. Spoon chicken mixture into 9-inch pie plate and top with 4 refrigerated biscuits. Bake 15 minutes or until biscuits are golden.

Sunday Hash

A box of hash brown potatoes is a meal waiting for the meaty accent of provolone or salami.

SERVES 4.

1   tablespoon olive oil
1   box (6 ounces) hash brown potatoes
8   ounces smoked, hard sausage, sliced $1/4$ inch thick
2   tablespoons margarine
      Salt to taste

ADD A TOUCH:
Spoon $1/2$ cup tomato salsa onto hash brown potatoes just before serving.

Heat oil in 12-inch skillet. Add hash brown potatoes, sausage, $1^1/2$ cups hot water, and margarine.

Cook over medium heat, stirring occasionally to brown potatoes, and allow water to evaporate, about 10 minutes. Season with salt to taste. Remove from heat and serve.

Tex-Mex Lasagna

You'll find precooked logs of polenta (cooked cornmeal) wherever pasta is sold. You can also make polenta using a quick-cooking mix.

SERVES 6.

1/2	pound chorizo
1	box (7 ounces) instant refried beans
1	roll (1 pound) prepared polenta, unflavored
1 1/2	cups shredded Mexican-style cheese
1	cup salsa

Preheat oven to 350 degrees F.

In 12-inch skillet, brown chorizo. Add beans and 1 3/4 cups hot water. Bring to a boil. Cover. Turn off heat and let sit 5 minutes.

Cut polenta into thick slices and arrange in bottom of greased 9-inch square pan. Spread with chorizo and bean mixture. Sprinkle with cheese. Bake 15 minutes. Remove from oven. Top with salsa and serve.

Cassoulet

Use kielbasa or any similar garlicky Middle European sausage to season this dish.

SERVES 4.

4	strips bacon
1	small onion, peeled and chopped
1	large carrot, peeled and chopped
4	skinless, boneless chicken thighs, cut into 1-inch pieces
1	package (9 ounces) smoked sausage, cut into 1-inch chunks
3	tablespoons tomato paste
1	box (6 to 7 ounces) seasoned bean medley

Preheat oven to 350 degrees F.

Brown bacon in large pot. Remove bacon and set aside. Add onion and carrot to bacon fat and sauté 5 minutes. Add chicken thighs and brown 5 minutes. Add sausage chunks, tomato paste, bean medley, and 3 cups water. Bring to a boil. Cook, uncovered, at medium heat 15 minutes.

Remove from heat, sprinkle on bacon, and serve.

Farm Sausage Bake

Serve this hearty dish as a weekend breakfast or quick dinner with Spinach-Orange Salad (see page 128).

SERVES 4.

1	package (12 ounces) Mexican-style cooked, seasoned ground beef
1	medium apple, cored, seeded, and finely chopped (peeling isn't necessary)
1	green bell pepper, cored, seeded, and finely chopped
2	cups herb-seasoned stuffing mix
3/4	cup or more chicken broth

Preheat oven to 350 degrees F.

In a bowl, stir together beef, apple, and green pepper. Stir in stuffing mix and 3/4 cup broth or enough to moisten mixture.

Spoon into 3-quart casserole. Bake 30 minutes or until hot and browned on top. Remove from oven and serve.

Variation: Spoon mixture into hollowed-out Rome Beauty apples. Place stuffed apples in shallow baking pan. Add about 10 minutes to baking time.

Southwestern Brunch Casserole

If you want a little more sleep time before your brunch guests arrive, assemble this dish and refrigerate up to one day in advance. Bake as directed.

SERVES 4 TO 6.

1	box (6 ounces) hash brown potatoes
1	cup frozen mixed corn and green peppers
1	can (11 ounces) nacho cheese soup
1	pound sage or maple-flavored pork sausage roll
1	cup shredded Mexican-style Cheddar cheese

Preheat oven to 325 degrees F.

Pour hash brown potatoes into 12-inch skillet. Prepare according to package directions, but do not brown. Stir in frozen vegetables and sauté 3 minutes or until thawed.

Stir ²/₃ of soup into potato mixture. Spoon potato mixture into well-greased 8-inch square ovenproof dish. Set aside.

In a large skillet, brown sausage, breaking up chunks with back of spoon. Pour off any fat. Spread sausage over potato mixture. Spoon remaining nacho cheese soup over sausage. Sprinkle on cheese.

Bake casserole 25 minutes or until cheese is well browned. Remove from oven and serve.

Italian Sausage-Polenta Casserole

If you keep a roll of polenta and a jar of pasta sauce in the cupboard, you'll never go hungry. Select a well-seasoned sauce to complement the subtle cornmeal.

SERVES 4 TO 6.

1	roll (1 pound) prepared polenta, unflavored
1	tablespoon olive oil
1	small onion, finely chopped
1	pound hot or mild Italian sausage
1	jar (28 ounces) mushroom-flavored pasta sauce

Preheat oven to 350 degrees F.

Cut polenta into 9 even slices. Arrange in bottom of well-greased, 9-inch square glass baking dish. Set aside.

Heat olive oil in large skillet. Add onion and sauté 5 minutes over medium heat. Add sausage, crumble with a spoon, and brown. Pour off any fat.

Stir pasta sauce into sausage mixture and heat 5 minutes.

Pour sausage mixture over polenta. Bake for 15 minutes or until thoroughly heated. Remove from oven and serve.

ADD A TOUCH:
Sprinkle with 1 cup grated Asiago cheese before baking.

Mashed Potato Pie

SERVES 6.

1	box (5.5 ounces) mashed potato buds
2/3	cup milk
1/4	cup butter
1	teaspoon salt
3	eggs, beaten
1/2	cup grated Italian cheese blend
4	teaspoons Dijon-style mustard
1/2	teaspoon pepper
1	(9-inch) deep-dish piecrust, unbaked

Preheat oven to 400 degrees F.

To prepare mashed potatoes, combine potato buds, 2 2/3 cups water, milk, butter, and salt in medium-size pot. Bring to a boil. Add eggs, cheese, mustard, and pepper. Beat well.

Spoon potato mixture into piecrust. Bake for 50 minutes or until potatoes are golden and knife inserted near center comes out clean. Remove from oven. Let sit for 5 minutes before slicing.

meals-in-one

skillet dinners

Chicken Florentine

When using frozen spinach in a recipe, there's no need to thaw the vegetable first, but break up the frozen block as it cooks for even doneness.

SERVES 4.

1	tablespoon butter
1	box (10 ounces) roasted, sliced chicken breast
1	box (4 ounces) noodles stroganoff
1	box (9 ounces) frozen, chopped spInach
1	cup milk
2	tablespoons sour cream
1/4	cup grated Parmesan cheese

Melt butter in 12-inch skillet. Add chicken, noodles stroganoff, and spinach. Add 1 cup water and milk. Bring to a simmer. Cook over low heat 8 minutes or until noodles are tender. Stir in sour cream and cheese. Remove from heat and serve.

Chicken "Rice Bowl"

Combine rice, vegetables, and chicken in one dish for one of the most popular entrées you can assemble.

SERVES 4.

1	tablespoon margarine
1	box (6.2 ounces) chicken-flavored rice and pasta
1	box (10 ounces) roasted, sliced chicken breast
1	tablespoon soy sauce
1	tablespoon lime juice
1/2	cup minced scallions
1	pinch crushed red pepper flakes

ADD A TOUCH:
Stir in 1 package
(9 ounces) frozen
snow peas with
the chicken.

Melt margarine in 12-inch skillet. Add rice and pasta mix (reserve seasoning mix from box) and sauté 1 minute. Add 2¼ cups water. Bring to a boil. Reduce heat to low. Cover and simmer 8 minutes or until rice is tender.

Stir chicken into rice. Add seasoning mix from rice, soy sauce, lime juice, scallions, and red pepper flakes. Simmer 5 minutes or until rice is tender and liquid is absorbed. Remove from heat and serve.

Shrimp and Rice, Caribbean Style

Heighten the fresh fruit taste of this shrimp and rice dinner by garnishing each serving with diced tropical fruit, such as papaya, pineapple, or mango.

SERVES 4.

1	tablespoon olive oil
2	garlic cloves, minced
1	red bell pepper, cored, seeded, and diced
1	cup orange juice
1	box (8 ounces) yellow rice with seasonings
1	package (12 ounces) frozen, peeled, raw shrimp
1/2	cup sliced pimiento-stuffed olives

Heat oil in 12-inch skillet. Add garlic and bell pepper and sauté 5 minutes. Add juice and 1¼ cups water. Bring to a boil. Stir in rice and shrimp. Reduce heat, cover, and simmer until rice is tender, about 35 minutes. Stir in olives, remove from heat, and serve.

Chicken with Jasmine Rice

Although many mixes use dried herbs, you'll enhance the quality by adding fresh ones as well. Their aroma makes any dish more appealing.

SERVES 2.

1	tablespoon vegetable oil
1	cup sliced mushrooms
1	box (6.7 ounces) garlic-basil flavored jasmine rice
1½	cups chicken broth
1	box (6 ounces) roasted, sliced chicken breast
2	tablespoons chopped basil
2	tablespoons chopped scallions

ADD A TOUCH:
Stir in a dash of soy sauce at the end of cooking.

Heat oil in 12-inch skillet. Add mushrooms and sauté 2 to 3 minutes. Stir in jasmine rice and chicken broth. Bring to a boil. Reduce heat to low, cover, and simmer 10 minutes. Add chicken, cover, and simmer another 10 minutes or until rice is tender. Stir in basil and scallions. Remove from heat and serve.

Chicken Risotto

This Italian stirred rice dish now comes packaged with flavorings. Just add fresh vegetables and some cream to enrich the dish.

SERVES 2 TO 3.

1	tablespoon olive oil
1	small onion, minced
1	cup sliced wild mushrooms
2	tablespoons dry white wine
1	package (6.3 ounces) chicken and Parmesan risotto mix

Heat oil in 12-inch skillet. Add onion and mushrooms and sauté 5 minutes. Add white wine and cook 1 minute or until liquid evaporates. Add risotto mix and 2 cups water. Bring to a boil, stirring occasionally. Reduce heat to medium and cook, uncovered, 10 minutes or until rice is tender. Heat until thickened and hot. Remove from heat and serve.

Arroz Con Pollo

Well-flavored rice takes top billing in this Caribbean dish. Add plenty of vegetables for color.

SERVES 4.

1	tablespoon olive oil
1	package (10 ounces) frozen bell pepper strips and diced onions, unthawed
1	tomato, cored and diced
1	box (10.3 ounces) chicken flavored rice and vermicelli mix
1	box (10 ounces) roasted, sliced chicken breast
1	cup frozen, thawed peas

Heat oil in 12-inch skillet. Add bell pepper and onion mixture and sauté over medium heat 5 minutes. Stir in tomato and rice mix. Add 3½ cups water. Bring to a boil. Stir in chicken and peas. Reduce heat to low, cover, and simmer 15 minutes. Remove from heat and serve.

Chicken and Mushroom Skillet Dinner

Choose oyster or shiitake mushrooms or opt for packaged mixed, wild mushrooms if your supermarket carries the product.

SERVES 4.

2	tablespoons olive oil
2	cups sliced mushrooms
1	box (10 ounces) roasted, sliced chicken breast
1	can (10.75 ounces) golden mushroom soup
1	teaspoon paprika
1/2	teaspoon salt
1/2	teaspoon pepper
2	cups instant rice

Heat olive oil in 12-inch nonstick skillet. Add mushrooms and sauté 5 minutes.

Add chicken, mushroom soup, paprika, salt, and pepper. Add 1½ cups water and bring to a boil. Stir in rice. Cover and simmer until rice is tender, about 5 minutes. Remove from heat and serve.

Chicken Cacciatore

Be sure to accompany this dish with pasta, rice, or mashed potatoes to soak up the savory sauce.

SERVES 4.

1	tablespoon olive oil
1	package (4 ounces) sliced mushrooms
2	boxes (10 ounces each) cooked, sliced chicken breast
1	jar (28 ounces) pasta sauce with basil and garlic
1	tablespoon roasted-garlic salad-dressing mix
1/2	teaspoon salt
1/4	teaspoon pepper

ADD A TOUCH:
Stir in 1/2 cup pitted kalamata olives and 1 teaspoon fresh, minced thyme.

Heat olive oil in 12-inch skillet. Add mushrooms and sauté 5 minutes. Stir in remaining ingredients. Simmer 10 minutes for flavors to blend and mixture to heat through. Remove from heat and serve.

Tex-Mex Eggs

Eggs are not just for breakfast anymore. This spicy scramble of beef, tortilla chips, and eggs is a great weeknight dinner or brunch entrée.

SERVES 4.

1	tablespoon vegetable oil
1	box (12 ounces) precooked Mexican-seasoned ground beef
1	cup chopped tomato
8	eggs
1/2	cup chopped scallions
1/2	teaspoon salt
1/2	teaspoon pepper
1	cup crumbled tortilla chips
1	cup grated Cheddar cheese

Heat oil in 12-inch nonstick skillet. Add beef and tomato and sauté 5 minutes or until meat is hot.

Meanwhile, in large bowl, beat together eggs, scallions, salt, and pepper. Pour over meat and scramble gently over low-medium heat until almost set. Stir in tortilla chips and let the eggs set. Sprinkle on cheese. Remove from heat and serve.

ADD A TOUCH:
Spoon 1 tablespoon each of sour cream and salsa over each serving.

Cajun Red Beans and Rice

You'll find andouille (ahn-DO-ee) sausage, a firm and highly spiced meat mixture, in high-end supermarkets. You can substitute a highly seasoned kielbasa sausage if necessary.

SERVES 4.

1	tablespoon vegetable oil
1	small onion, finely chopped
1	package (10 ounces) andouille sausage, sliced 1/2 inch thick
1	can (14.5 ounces) diced tomatoes with green chiles
1	box (8 ounces) red beans and rice

Heat vegetable oil in large skillet. Add onion and sauté 5 minutes over medium heat. Add sausage and heat 1 minute. Stir in tomatoes and 1½ cups water. Stir in red beans and rice. Bring mixture to boil. Reduce heat to low, cover, and simmer 30 minutes, stirring occasionally or until beans and rice are tender. Remove from heat and serve.

Country Ham and Noodle Dinner

If you can't find a package of diced ham in your supermarket, choose a thick slice of precooked ham and cut it into chunks.

SERVES 4.

2	packages (5 ounces each) Romanoff noodle mix
1	cup milk
2	tablespoons butter
1	package (9 ounces) frozen baby peas
1	package (1 pound) diced, cooked ham
1/2	cup chopped scallions
1/2	cup sour cream

To prepare noodles, combine noodle mix, 2½ cups water, milk, and butter in 5-quart pot. Add peas and bring to a boil.

Remove from heat and allow to thicken, 2 to 3 minutes. Stir in ham, scallions, and sour cream and serve.

Jambalaya

Use either plain or flavored instant rice for jambalaya. You'll find plenty of vegetable and herb rice blends to choose from.

SERVES 4.

1	tablespoon vegetable oil
1	large celery stalk, trimmed and diced
1	can (14 ounces) stewed tomatoes
4	cups diced, cooked ham
1	can (14 to 16 ounces) chicken broth
1/4	to 1/2 teaspoon crushed red pepper flakes*
1	box (7 ounces) instant rice

ADD A TOUCH:
Stir in 1 cup cooked shrimp with ham.

Heat oil in 12-inch skillet. Add celery. Sauté 5 minutes over medium heat. Add tomatoes, ham, chicken broth, and red pepper flakes. Bring to a boil. Stir in rice. Cover skillet.

Remove from heat and let stand 5 minutes or until rice is tender and liquid is absorbed.

*1/4 teaspoon crushed red pepper flakes is mildly hot; 1/2 teaspoon is quite steamy.

Thai Noodle and Shrimp Dinner

The opaque white rice noodles cook very quickly, so watch the pot. Overcooking results in mushy texture.

SERVES 4.

1	box (7 ounces) wide rice noodles
1	tablespoon vegetable oil
1	bag (16 ounces) frozen, thawed cooked, peeled shrimp
3	to 4 tablespoons teriyaki sauce
1/4	cup finely chopped scallions

Bring 4-quart pot of water to boil. Add rice noodles. Boil 3 minutes or until just tender. Drain and set aside.

Meanwhile, heat vegetable oil in large skillet. Add shrimp and heat through. Add noodles to skillet. Toss with 3 tablespoons teriyaki sauce. (Add additional tablespoon if necessary to coat all ingredients.) Remove from heat, sprinkle with scallions, and serve.

ADD A TOUCH:
Sprinkle 1/4 cup chopped cashews or peanuts over the dish before serving.

Thai Noodle and Tofu Dinner

You'll find stir-fry sauces in varying degrees of heat. Select a product with a kick to compensate for the bland tofu.

SERVES 4.

1	box (7 ounces) wide rice noodles
2	tablespoons vegetable oil, divided
1	package (1 pound) fresh or frozen and thawed vegetables for stir-fry
1	pound firm tofu, drained and cut into 1/2-inch cubes
2/3	cup stir-fry sauce

Bring 4-quart pot of water to boil. Add rice noodles. Boil 3 minutes or until just tender. Drain and set aside.

Meanwhile, heat 1 tablespoon vegetable oil in large wok or skillet. Add vegetables and stir-fry 2 to 3 minutes. Remove. Add remaining oil to wok and heat. Add tofu. Stand back, as tofu may sizzle. Cook 2 minutes.

Return vegetables to skillet. Add noodles. Pour in stir-fry sauce and heat through. Remove from heat and serve.

Variation: Instead of using noodles, prepare 2 cups instant rice. Spoon vegetable and tofu mixture over rice to serve.

meals-in-one

stews

Chicken Stew with Biscuits

SERVES 8.

1	package (5.9 ounces) hearty chicken noodle soup mix
1	package (10 ounces) frozen, mixed vegetables
1	box (10 ounces) roasted, sliced chicken breast
8	baking-powder biscuits or dinner rolls

Combine soup mix with 6 cups water in 5-quart pot. Add vegetables. Bring to a boil. Stir. Reduce heat to low and add chicken. Simmer until slightly thickened, about 5 minutes.

Serve in bowls with biscuits on the side.

Country Captain

According to some food historians, British sea traders brought this dish from India to the Southern United States in colonial days.

SERVES 4.

1	tablespoon vegetable oil
1	small onion, diced
1	box (1.8 ounces) tomato-beef flavor soup mix
1/2	cup yellow raisins
1	teaspoon curry powder
1	can (14 ounces) diced tomatoes
1	box (10 ounces) roasted, sliced chicken breast
2	cups cooked instant rice

ADD A TOUCH:
Buy a good-quality mango chutney and pass separately.

Heat oil in 12-inch skillet. Add onion and sauté 5 minutes. Stir in soup mix, 1/2 cup water, raisins, curry powder, and diced tomatoes with liquid. Bring to a boil. Reduce heat to low. Stir in chicken and heat through.

To serve, spoon over 1/2 cup cooked rice and top with chicken sauce.

Pennsylvania Dutch Chicken with Noodles

When your family needs to defrost from the cold, make this dish that's half soup, half stew, and totally satisfying.

SERVES 4.

1	package (3.14 ounces) cream of vegetable soup mix
1	cup milk
1	package (9 ounces) frozen mixed vegetables
1	box (6 ounces) roasted, sliced chicken breast
2	cups cooked egg noodles

Combine soup mix, milk, and 2 cups water. Bring to a boil. Add frozen vegetables and chicken.

Reduce heat to low and simmer, uncovered, 5 minutes, stirring frequently, or until thick and smooth. Stir in egg noodles and heat through. Remove from heat and serve.

ADD A TOUCH:
Serve in hollowed-out sourdough bread bowls.

Beef in Picadillo Sauce

The combination of hot and sweet ingredients makes this Mexican-inspired beef dish special.

SERVES 4.

1	box (1 pound) cooked beef roast
1	tablespoon olive oil
1	small onion, chopped
1/4	teaspoon ground cinnamon
1/2	teaspoon chili powder
1	can (14 to 15 ounces) crushed tomatoes
1/4	cup sliced pimiento-stuffed olives
1/4	cup raisins

ADD A TOUCH:
Serve with a box
of prepared
Spanish rice.

Drain and reserve juice from beef. Thinly slice beef.

In 12-inch skillet, heat oil. Add onion, cinnamon, and chili powder and cook over low heat 3 minutes. Stir in tomatoes, olives, raisins, and juice from beef package. Simmer 5 minutes. Add beef and simmer 5 more minutes or until hot. Remove from heat and serve.

Old-Fashioned Beef Stew

Vary this stew to your taste by selecting Italian or Asian mixed frozen vegetables.

SERVES 4.

1	tablespoon olive oil
1	pound beef strips for stir-fry*
1	package (10 ounces) frozen bell pepper strips and diced onions, unthawed
3	cups refrigerated, diced potatoes with onion (from a 20-ounce package)
1	box (1.8 ounces) tomato-beef soup, dip, and recipe mix
1	tablespoon Worcestershire sauce

Heat oil in Dutch oven. Add half the beef strips at a time. Don't crowd. Brown 1 minute per side. Remove.

Add bell pepper and onion mixture, potato and onion mixture, tomato-beef soup, Worcestershire sauce, and 2 cups water to Dutch oven. Bring to a boil. Reduce heat to low. Return beef to pot. Cover and simmer 15 minutes or until stew is thick and meat is tender.

*Many supermarket meat counters sell sliced flank steak for stir-fry. Otherwise, slice 1 pound flank or round steak into $1/4$-inch-thick strips.

Thirty-Minute Beef Goulash

SERVES 6.

2	tablespoons olive oil
1	medium onion, chopped
2	large Portobello mushrooms, chopped (or 1 cup chopped white mushrooms)
1	package (17 ounces) refrigerated beef roast au jus*
1	package (1 pound) refrigerated cooked, diced, seasoned red-skin potatoes**
1	can (12 ounces) beef broth
1	teaspoon hot paprika
1/2	teaspoon pepper

ADD A TOUCH:
Top each serving with a dollop of sour cream.

Heat oil in large pot. Add onion and mushrooms and sauté 5 minutes over medium heat.

Open package of beef and cut into bite-size pieces. Add beef and gravy to pot. Stir in remaining ingredients.

Bring to a boil. Reduce heat to medium and cook 10 minutes or until mixture is hot and slightly thickened. Remove from heat and serve.

*This should be found in the wide variety of precooked beef items in supermarket meat counters. Choose a product that is packaged with a seasoned gravy to save you cooking steps.

**You'll find precooked, seasoned potatoes in the produce section of your supermarket. Store these in the refrigerator as you would other cooked vegetables.

meals-in-one

Vegetable-Ham Stew

Use any brand of hearty or kettle-type soup for this stew. The words "cream of" are your clue that the dish will be thick textured.

SERVES 6.

1	packet (3.14 ounces) cream of vegetable soup mix or 1 cup cream of vegetable soup mix
3	cups milk
1	package (1 pound) diced ham
1	package (1 pound) frozen Italian-style vegetables

Combine soup mix and milk in large pot. Bring to a boil, stirring frequently.

Reduce heat to low. Stir in ham and vegetables. Cover and simmer 20 minutes. Remove from heat and serve.

Sweet-Hot Pork

*The robust smoky flavor of Southern barbecue is captured in a
simple salsa and jam glaze for pork.*

SERVES 4.

1	box (1 pound) cooked pork cubes
2	tablespoons taco seasoning mix
1	jar (16 ounces) salsa*
1/3	cup apricot jam or orange marmalade

ADD A TOUCH:
Serve over cooked
instant rice.

In a large skillet, combine all ingredients. Simmer 5 minutes or until heated
through. Remove from heat and serve.

*Choose medium to hot salsa, according to taste.

Provençal Pork Stew with Sour Cream Mashed Potatoes

Use pasta sauce straight from the jar or add your own vegetable and herb touches. Mushrooms, artichoke hearts, olives, capers, and crumbled bacon are welcome additions.

SERVES 4.

1	box (1 pound) cooked pork cubes
2	tablespoons flour
2	tablespoons olive oil
1	jar (26 ounces) garlic-flavored pasta sauce
1	can (8 ounces) artichoke hearts, drained and quartered
1	box (7.6 ounces) sour cream and chive mashed potato mix

Coat pork cubes with flour.

Pour oil into 10-inch skillet. Add pork and brown on all sides. Add pasta sauce and artichoke hearts. Simmer 10 minutes.

Prepare mashed potatoes according to package directions and spoon the mashed potatoes onto four plates. Top with pork and sauce.

Shrimp Gumbo

If you're not a fan of okra, substitute a package of the frozen mixed vegetables of your choice.

SERVES 4.

1	box (7 ounces) gumbo mix with rice
1	package (10 ounces) frozen, sliced okra
1	package (12 ounces) frozen cooked shrimp
1	tablespoon lemon juice

In a 5-quart pot, combine gumbo mix and 5 cups water. Bring to boil.

Reduce heat, cover, and simmer 10 minutes. Stir in okra and shrimp. Cover and simmer another 5 to 10 minutes or until rice is tender. Remove from heat, stir in lemon juice, and serve.

in the dough: breakfast and brunch foods, sandwiches, pizzas, and focaccia

Basil, Tomato, and Mozzarella Shortcake

Prepare this delicate sandwich during the summer when markets are filled with the aroma of basil.

SERVES 4.

4   baking-powder biscuits
2   tablespoons mayonnaise,
            divided
2   medium tomatoes, sliced thin
            Fresh basil leaves

ADD A TOUCH:
Add a slice of mozzarella cheese with tomatoes.

Split each biscuit in half.

Spread 1½ teaspoons mayonnaise on bottom half of each biscuit. Top with several tomato slices and arrange 3 or 4 large basil leaves over tomatoes. Cover with top half of biscuit and serve.

Double Blueberry Brunch Sandwiches

For a tempting brunch dessert, substitute ½ cup vanilla ice cream for the ricotta cheese filling.

SERVES 6.

1	carton (1 pound) ricotta cheese
¼	teaspoon ground cinnamon
1	tablespoon sugar
12	frozen blueberry waffles
3	cups blueberry sauce or blueberry pie filling

Preheat oven to 400 degrees F.

In a bowl, stir together ricotta cheese, cinnamon, and sugar.

Place waffles on cookie sheet. Bake 6 to 8 minutes or until hot and lightly browned.

Spread ⅓ cup ricotta cheese mixture on 6 waffles. Top with second waffle. Spoon ½ cup blueberry sauce over each serving.

Cheese Quesadillas with Apple Pie Topping

Apple pie topped with a wedge of cheese is delicious. This dish of cheese with a topping of apples turns the duo upside down.

SERVES 6.

6	(6- to 8-inch) flour tortillas
1	package (8 ounces) shredded Italian cheese blend
2	tablespoons butter, divided
1	can (21 ounces) apple pie filling

Working with one flour tortilla at a time, sprinkle on a scant ⅓ cup cheese. Fold tortilla in half. Repeat with remaining tortillas and cheese.

Melt half the butter in 10-inch skillet. Arrange 2 folded tortillas in skillet. Fry 3 minutes on first side, turn over with spatula, and fry 2 minutes on second side until golden on both sides. Remove.

Cut each tortilla in half to form 2 quarters. Add more butter as necessary and fry remaining tortillas.

To serve, arrange 2 quesadillas on each of 6 plates. Top each with a dollop of apple pie filling.

Stuffed French Toast

Make this delightful breakfast sandwich for a weekend breakfast or brunch. Arrange the sandwiches ahead of time, wrap, and chill. Bake as needed.

SERVES 3.

6	slices frozen home-style French toast
1	package (3 ounces) cream cheese, at room temperature
1/4	cup pear or apple butter

Preheat oven to 400 degrees F.

Generously spread 3 slices French toast with cream cheese. Spread remaining 3 slices French toast with fruit butter. Close to make sandwiches.

Place sandwiches on cookie sheet. Bake for 15 minutes or until golden brown, crisp, and hot. Remove from oven and serve.

in the dough

Sausage en Croute with Cranberry Chutney

Inspired by the 1950s appetizer "pigs in a blanket," this dish is updated with mustard and chutney.

SERVES 6.

1	can (15.5 ounces) refrigerated crescent rolls (6 dinner rolls)
1	package (1 pound) kielbasa links (6 links)
3	tablespoons hot-sweet mustard
2	cups fruit chutney

Preheat oven to 350 degrees F.

Unwrap package of rolls. Separate into individual rolls. Place one roll in front of you so the point faces away and the base of the triangular roll is closest to you. Arrange one kielbasa link across the base. Spread with 1½ teaspoons mustard. Roll up kielbasa and dough toward tip. Pinch to seal. Place on ungreased cookie sheet. Repeat with remaining dough, sausages, and mustard. Bake for 20 minutes or until dough is golden brown.

To serve, place 1 sausage on each of 6 plates. Serve chutney on the side.

Empanadas

Every country has its version of meat patties. The South American empanada is distinguished by its fruity and spicy taste.

SERVES 4.

1	box (15 ounces) prepared piecrust (2 crusts)
1	package (12 ounces) Mexican-style cooked, seasoned ground beef
1/4	cup raisins
1/4	cup chopped walnuts
1	cup shredded Mexican-style or sharp Cheddar cheese

Preheat oven to 400 degrees F.

Unfold both piecrusts and place on cookie sheet. Spread half the ground beef on half of each piecrust to form half a circle. Sprinkle each with half the raisins and walnuts. Leave 1 inch of border of crust clear. Sprinkle each with ½ cup cheese.

Fold piecrust in half to enclose filling. Press edges with tines of fork to seal. Bake 16 to 18 minutes or until crusts are golden. Cut each empanada in half to serve.

in the dough

Roast Beef and Cheddar Sandwiches

You don't have to wait for Sunday night's leftovers to enjoy a two-fisted roast beef sandwich. Serve this with coleslaw or potato salad.

SERVES 4.

1	box (16 ounces) cooked beef pot roast
1/4	cup steak sauce
1	can (10.75 ounces) condensed Cheddar cheese or nacho Cheddar soup
4	kaiser rolls

Slice beef 1/4 inch thick. Place beef slices and package juices in skillet. Add steak sauce. Simmer 5 minutes to thoroughly heat.

Pour soup into small pot and heat.

To assemble, cut rolls in half. On bottom half of each, layer on one-quarter of the beef and melted cheese. Close with top half of rolls and serve.

Mediterranean Tostadas

Who says you can't mix Mexican tostadas with an Italian filling?
This blend of ethnic flavors makes a great lunch or snack.

SERVES 4.

1	package (8 ounces) hot Italian sausage
3/4	cup pasta sauce
8	corn tostada shells
1	cup grated mozzarella cheese

Preheat oven to 400 degrees F.

Brown sausage in skillet, breaking up chunks with back of spoon. Add pasta sauce and simmer 2 minutes or until hot.

Place 4 corn tostada shells on cookie sheet. Top each with $^1/_2$ cup sausage mixture. Add second tostada. Sprinkle each with $^1/_4$ cup grated cheese. Bake for 6 to 8 minutes or until cheese melts and mixture is hot. Remove from oven and serve.

Ten-Minute Tacos

Place bowls of hot seasoned ground beef, Cheddar, guacamole, and lettuce on the table and let the family build their own tacos.

SERVES 4.

1	tablespoon vegetable oil
1	small onion, chopped
1	box (12 ounces) Mexican-style cooked, seasoned ground beef
8	corn taco shells
1/2	cup shredded Cheddar cheese
1	cup shredded Romaine lettuce
1	package (16 ounces) prepared guacamole

Preheat oven to 350 degrees F.

Heat oil in large skillet. Add onion and sauté 2 to 3 minutes. Add cooked ground beef and heat 2 minutes. Set aside.

Arrange 8 taco shells on cookie sheet. Heat in oven 3 minutes.

Divide meat mixture among taco shells. Top each with 1 tablespoon cheese and 2 tablespoons lettuce. Serve guacamole on the side.

Roast Beef Wrap

Fill a tortilla with roast beef, lettuce, and dressing, and you have a salad and sandwich in one. Use blue cheese or any chunky dressing you prefer.

SERVES 4.

1	box (1 pound) refrigerated, cooked, sliced roast beef
4	(10- to 12-inch) flour tortillas
4	Romaine lettuce leaves
1	cup thick and creamy blue cheese dressing

ADD A TOUCH:
Add sliced roasted red peppers to the wrap. Substitute your own leftover roast beef if available.

Place beef on microwave-safe platter. Heat 1 minute at high power. Remove from oven. Divide beef among tortillas. Top each serving with one lettuce leaf and ¼ cup dressing.

Fold bottom of tortilla up to center, then fold sides in to wrap the filling.

Reuben Smothered with Slaw

A sandwich is still one of America's favorite meals, especially when it's the stick-to-the-ribs Reuben.

SERVES 4.

1/4	cup hot-sweet or Dijon-style mustard
8	slices pumpernickel bread
1	package (8 ounces) sliced corned beef
1	package (8 ounces) sliced Swiss cheese
1	package (16 ounces) prepared cole slaw*
1/4	cup butter

For each sandwich, spread 1 tablespoon mustard on each of 4 slices bread. Top each with 2 ounces corned beef and a slice or two of Swiss cheese. Spread with ½ cup coleslaw. Top with second bread slice.

Melt 2 tablespoons butter in 10-inch skillet. Add 2 sandwiches. Sauté 3 to 4 minutes per side or until cheese melts and bread is crisp. Repeat with remaining 2 tablespoons butter and remaining 2 sandwiches. Cut each sandwich in half to serve.

*You'll find prepared cole slaw in supermarket deli cases.

Chicken Fajitas

When adding salsa to a sandwich, drain off any excess liquid first so you don't get a soggy mess.

SERVES 4.

1	tablespoon vegetable oil
1	medium onion, peeled and thinly sliced
1	box (10 ounces) roasted, sliced chicken breast cut into bite-size pieces
1	package (1.2 ounces) fajita mix
4	(8- to 10-inch) flour tortillas
1/2	cup grated Mexican cheese blend
1/4	cup salsa
1	cup shredded lettuce

Heat oil in 10-inch skillet. Add onion. Sauté 5 minutes or until tender. Stir in chicken. Add fajita mix and ¼ cup water. Heat through.

Arrange tortillas on work surface. Divide chicken mixture among tortillas. Top each with 2 tablespoons cheese, 1 tablespoon salsa, and ¼ cup lettuce. Fold to encase filling and serve.

Pepper and Sausage Calzone

As a convenience, you can assemble this pocket sandwich up to a day in advance and refrigerate. Remove the calzone from the refrigerator while you preheat the oven.

SERVES 4.

1	pound Italian sausage, hot or mild
1	can (15 ounces) pizza sauce
1	cup frozen red bell pepper and onion strips
1	(12- to 13-inch) frozen pizza crust, thawed

Preheat oven to 375 degrees F.

In 12-inch skillet, brown sausage, breaking up chunks with back of spoon. Pour off fat. Stir in pizza sauce, and peppers and onions.

Place crust on work surface. Spoon meat sauce over one side of crust, leaving the other side clear. Fold crust over to enclose filling. Press edges with tines of fork to seal.

Place in greased jelly roll pan. Make 2 or 3 slashes in top of calzone for steam to escape. Bake 20 minutes or until golden. Remove from oven and let set 5 minutes to firm up. Slice and serve.

ADD A TOUCH:
Sprinkle 1 cup grated mozzarella cheese over filling before folding.

Pulled Pork Sandwich

Hot pork barbecue is great fare for a football tailgate party. Heat the pork, then pack in a vacuum container to keep warm.

SERVES 8.

1	package (2 pounds) cooked, barbecue shredded pork
1/4	teaspoon crushed red pepper flakes*
1	quart prepared cole slaw**
8	sandwich buns

Combine pork and crushed red pepper flakes in a small pot. Simmer 5 minutes to heat.

To assemble sandwiches, add ½ cup pork to bottom half of each roll. Top with ½ cup coleslaw and close sandwich with top half of roll.

*¹/₄ teaspoon crushed red pepper flakes is mildly hot; ¹/₂ teaspoon is quite steamy.

**You'll find prepared cole slaw in supermarket deli cases.

in the dough

Sloppy Joe Pizza

Instead of putting Sloppy Joe sauce on a bun, spread it on a pizza crust. Heap on the cheese and bake.

SERVES 4 TO 6.

1	box (12 ounces) Mexican-style cooked, seasoned ground beef
1	can (14 to 15 ounces) Sloppy Joe sauce
1	(12-inch) prepared thick pizza crust
1	tablespoon olive oil
2	cups shredded Cheddar cheese or 1 cup shredded Cheddar and 1 cup shredded Italian cheese blend

Preheat oven to 425 degrees F.

Place cooked beef in bowl. Stir in Sloppy Joe sauce.

Place pizza crust on cookie sheet. Brush with olive oil. Spread with meat sauce. Sprinkle with cheese. Bake for 12 minutes or until cheese melts and meat topping is hot. Remove from heat and serve.

Roast Vegetable Pizza

Restaurants roast vegetables to create their mouthwatering pizza creations. You can eliminate this step using convenient frozen vegetables.

SERVES 4.

1   box (14 ounces) frozen roast vegetables*
1   (12- to 14-inch) prepared pizza crust, frozen or refrigerated

Preheat oven to 425 degrees F.

Sprinkle frozen vegetables over pizza crust, and place on cookie sheet.

Bake 12 to 15 minutes or until vegetables are hot.

*Choose a variety of roast vegetables that do not contain a lot of potatoes.

BLT Focaccia

Form crescent rolls into a thick, focaccia-like crust and top with bacon, lettuce, and tomato for an open-faced sandwich.

SERVES 4.

1	container (8 ounces) reduced-fat crescent rolls
1/4	cup mayonnaise (reduced-fat mayonnaise is fine)
3	to 4 medium tomatoes, sliced 1/4 inch thick
1	package (about 12 ounces) precooked bacon, diced
1	cup shredded Romaine lettuce

Preheat oven to 375 degrees F.

Unroll crescent rolls but do not separate. Place on greased cookie sheet in one flat piece. Spread mayonnaise over dough. Arrange tomato slices over mayonnaise to cover dough. Sprinkle bacon over tomatoes.

Bake for 11 to 13 minutes or until dough is browned. Remove from oven and sprinkle on lettuce. Cut into 4 portions and serve.

salads and sides

Caesar Pasta Salad

Substitute a mixture of broccoli, carrots, and snow peas for the usual romaine lettuce of a Caesar salad.

SERVES 6.

1	bag (1 pound) refrigerated stir-fry vegetables
1	box (16 ounces) rotini or similar pasta, cooked and drained
$1/2$	cup Italian-Parmesan or Caesar salad dressing
$1/2$	teaspoon black pepper

Puncture vegetable bag in several places. Microwave vegetables on high heat for 5 minutes.

Spoon vegetables into serving bowl. Add cooked pasta and salad dressing. Sprinkle on pepper. Toss well and serve.

Tuscan Bread Salad

Toasted, cheesy croutons are the delicious base for a hearty salad. For a little variety, vary the flavor of the croutons.

SERVES 4.

1	box (5 ounces) or 3 cups Parmesan cheese croutons
2	medium tomatoes, cored and diced
1/4	cup chopped red onion
1/4	cup chopped fresh basil
1/3	cup bottled Italian dressing

ADD A TOUCH:

To turn this into an entrée, top with 1 box (10 ounces) roasted, sliced chicken breast or any leftover beef or pork strips.

Place croutons in a colander. Sprinkle with 2 tablespoons water to soften. Pour croutons into a bowl. Add tomatoes, red onion, and basil.

Pour dressing over salad mixture. Toss well.

Tortellini Salad

Use dry tortellini, available in the pasta section of supermarkets, or choose the quicker-cooking refrigerated variety.

SERVES 4.

1	box (about 12 ounces) cheese tortellini with cream sauce
2	tablespoons pesto
1/4	cup finely chopped chives
1	celery stalk, trimmed and chopped

Fill 3-quart pot with water and bring to a boil. Stir in tortellini, reserving cream sauce. Boil 8 minutes or until tender. Drain well and pour into serving bowl. Stir in 3 tablespoons cream sauce from package, pesto, chives, and celery. Toss gently and serve.

Tuna and Macaroni Salad

As if tuna weren't convenient enough, you'll now find it in foil packets paired with mayonnaise. You may substitute a can of water-packed tuna and mayonnaise or salad dressing to taste.

SERVES 4.

1	teaspoon salt, plus salt to taste
2	cups macaroni
1	box (12 ounces) tuna salad kit
1/4	cup chopped onion
1	cup chopped celery
1	tablespoon fresh lemon juice

ADD A TOUCH:
Stir in 1 cup chopped red bell pepper and 1 tablespoon capers.

Fill 3-quart pot with water, add 1 teaspoon salt, and bring to boil. Stir in macaroni. Cook at medium heat 12 minutes or until macaroni is tender. Drain well.

Pour macaroni into salad bowl. Open tuna kit. Add tuna and mayonnaise. Stir in onion, celery, and lemon juice. Add salt to taste and serve.

salads and sides

Zesty Potato-Onion Salad

You can never serve potato salad often enough to satisfy your family, especially when it's so easy.

SERVES 4 TO 6.

1	package (1 pound) cooked, diced potatoes and onions
1	cup diced celery
1	medium red bell pepper, cored, seeded, and diced
1/4	cup chopped scallion or red onion
2/3	cup mayonnaise-mustard dressing

Bring 6 quarts water to a boil. Add potatoes and cook 5 minutes to heat through. Drain thoroughly and place in serving bowl. Add celery, pepper, and scallions.

Spoon dressing over salad. Toss gently and serve.

Tuna Nicoise

This piquant French version of tuna salad also makes a great sandwich when you pack the tuna combination into 4 pita bread halves.

SERVES 4.

1	large tomato, cored, seeded, and diced
1	box (12 ounces) tuna salad kit
1	cup precooked, refrigerated, diced potatoes
1	tablespoon capers
2	cups baby mixed greens

In a bowl, combine tomato and tuna. Add dressing from kit.

Place potatoes in a small pot with water to cover. Bring to a boil. Reduce heat to simmer and cook 5 minutes. Drain well and add to tuna. Stir in capers.

To serve, place ½ cup baby mixed greens on each of 4 plates. Divide tuna mixture among plates.

Chicken and Wild Rice Salad

You can make this salad the day after Thanksgiving using leftover turkey instead of chicken.

SERVES 4.

1	box (2.75 ounces) quick-cooking wild rice
1	box (6 ounces) roasted, sliced chicken breast
¼	cup sliced almonds
¼	cup dried cranberries
½	cup balsamic vinaigrette dressing

Bring 1½ cups water to boil in small pot. Add wild rice. Stir. Reduce heat to low, cover, and simmer 5 minutes. Drain off excess liquid.

Place rice in serving bowl. Add chicken, almonds, and cranberries.

Pour dressing over salad. Toss gently and serve.

Holy Guacamole Salad

If your family shuns salads, you'll change their minds when you serve this zesty combination of tasty ingredients.

SERVES 4.

1	can (15 ounces) kidney beans, drained and rinsed
1	medium tomato, diced
1	box (6 ounces) roasted, sliced chicken breast
1	medium, ripe avocado, peeled, seeded, and diced
1/4	cup prepared French dressing
2	teaspoons taco seasoning mix
1	cup coarsely crumbled tortilla chips

ADD A TOUCH:
Instead of adding crumbled tortilla chips to the salad, serve the mixture in preformed tortilla bowls, available in many supermarkets.

In a bowl, stir together beans, tomato, chicken, and avocado.

In a cup, stir together dressing and taco seasoning mix. Pour over salad. Toss gently. Add tortilla chips. Toss again and serve.

Couscous and Beef Salad

Couscous, grains of semolina, don't need cooking. Just soak couscous in boiling water and proceed with your recipe.

SERVES 4.

1/2	teaspoon salt
1	box (10 ounces) couscous
1/2	cup bottled Italian dressing
1	medium tomato, cored and chopped
1/3	cup chopped fresh mint leaves
1/2	teaspoon pepper
1	box (1 pound) refrigerated, seasoned beef sirloin roast

Combine 2 cups water and salt in medium-size pot. Bring to a boil. Stir in couscous. Cover and set aside 5 minutes. Fluff with a fork. Spoon into a bowl. Add dressing, tomato, mint, and pepper to couscous. Stir and set aside.

Microwave beef roast according to package directions. Slice meat into 1/2-inch-thick strips. Discard beef juices. Add beef to salad, toss gently, and serve.

Spinach-Orange Salad

This vitamin-packed salad sports a sweet-and-sour dressing that children and adults will love. To turn the side into a main course, add 1 bag (12 ounces) of frozen cooked shrimp, thawed.

SERVES 4.

1	bag (6 ounces) washed baby spinach leaves
1	can (11 ounces) Mandarin orange segments
1	box (about 2 to 4 ounces) plain or herb-flavored croutons
1/2	cup vinaigrette dressing

In a salad bowl, combine spinach, orange segments, and croutons. Add dressing, toss well, and serve.

Broccoli Slaw Salad

Instead of the usual cabbage, use sweet and crisp broccoli strands in a salad. You'll love the taste, and you'll be giving your family a vitamin-rich salad.

SERVES 4.

3^1/$_2$ cups (one-half an 8-ounce package) broccoli coleslaw
1   cup dry chow mein noodles
^{1}/$_3$ cup teriyaki-style salad dressing

In a bowl, combine broccoli and noodles.

Pour dressing over salad. Toss gently and serve.

Potato Latkes with Dill–Sour Cream Sauce

In Eastern Europe, these crisp, lacy pancakes were served as an accompaniment to roast duck, but latkes also make a welcome brunch entrée.

SERVES 4.

1	box (6 ounces) frozen hash brown potatoes, thawed
1	teaspoon salt
2	tablespoons olive oil, plus additional for frying
1	small onion, chopped
2	eggs
1/4	cup flour
1/4	teaspoon salt
1/4	teaspoon pepper
	Dill–Sour Cream Sauce (follows)

Pour hash browns into a large bowl. Cover with 4 cups hot water and 1 teaspoon salt. Set aside 5 minutes. Drain well and return to bowl.

Meanwhile, heat 1 tablespoon olive oil in 12-inch nonstick skillet. Sauté onion 5 minutes or until tender. Add onion to potatoes. Beat in eggs, flour, salt, and pepper.

Add 1 tablespoon olive oil to skillet. Pour ¼ cup of the mixture into hot oil and cook over medium-high heat 5 minutes on first side and 2 to 3 minutes on second. Remove and keep warm. Repeat with additional olive oil as needed to cook remaining batter. Serve with Dill–Sour Cream Sauce (follows).

Dill-Sour Cream Sauce

1 1/2	cups sour cream
4	teaspoons minced fresh dill
1/4	teaspoon salt
1	small garlic clove, minced (optional)

Combine ingredients in a bowl. Stir well.

Hash Brown Potatoes with Alfredo Sauce

Cheese and Alfredo sauce make a rich topping for hash browns.

SERVES 6.

1	package (1.6 ounces) Alfredo sauce mix
2	cups milk
1	tablespoon butter
1	cup shredded Cheddar cheese or Monterey Jack and Cheddar blend
1	box (6 ounces) frozen hash brown potatoes, thawed

Combine Alfredo sauce mix and milk in medium pot over medium-high heat. Stir well. Add butter. Bring to a boil over medium heat, stirring frequently. Reduce heat to low. Stir in cheese. Simmer 2 minutes or until smooth and thickened.

Meanwhile, cook hash browns according to package directions.

Divide hash browns evenly onto 6 plates and serve with Alfredo mixture.

Steamed Vegetables with Tangy Cheese Sauce

This vegetable dish is so satisfying and wholesome that you may want to serve it as a vegetarian entrée.

SERVES 6.

2	packages (16 ounces each) vegetable medley
1	can (10.75 ounces) condensed cheese soup
1/4	cup milk or half-and-half
1	teaspoon Dijon-style mustard

Puncture vegetable bags in several places. Microwave vegetables, in bags, on high heat for 5 minutes or until tender.

Meanwhile, combine cheese soup, milk, and mustard in a small pot. Heat over low heat 5 minutes, stirring occasionally. To serve, spoon vegetables into serving dish. Top with cheese sauce mixture.

ADD A TOUCH:
Sprinkle toasted bread crumbs over the cheese sauce just before serving.

Corn Pudding

Serve this custard-like dish as a side to baked ham or chicken. You can even use it as a brunch entrée paired with a fruit salad.

SERVES 6.

1	package (1 pound) frozen corn or mixed vegetables with corn, thawed
3	eggs, beaten
1/2	cup butter, melted
1/2	cup milk
1	box (8.5 ounces) cornbread mix

Preheat oven to 350 degrees F.

In a bowl, stir together corn, eggs, butter, and milk. Stir in cornbread mix. Spoon into greased 2-quart baking dish. Bake 45 minutes or until firm but slightly creamy. Remove from oven and serve.

Asparagus and Rice

Prepare tender vegetables, such as asparagus or peas, with instant rice for a more satisfying side dish.

SERVES 4.

1	package (10 ounces) frozen, chopped asparagus
1¹/₄	cups instant rice
1	tablespoon butter
¹/₂	teaspoon salt
¹/₂	teaspoon pepper

Place asparagus in pot with 1¹/₂ cups water. Bring to a boil. Reduce heat to medium and cook 5 minutes. Stir in rice. Cover. Remove from heat and set aside 5 minutes. Stir in butter, salt, and pepper.

Variation: Substitute asparagus with 1 package (10 ounces) frozen peas.

ADD A TOUCH:
Add 1 teaspoon minced fresh dill to rice along with butter and seasonings.

desserts

Chocolate-Cherry Ice Cream Pie

To maintain the luscious texture of this pie, make and serve it the same day—which shouldn't be a problem.

SERVES 6 TO 8.

2	pints vanilla ice cream, softened
1	preformed graham cracker crust
1/2	cup chocolate fudge sauce
1	can (21 ounces) cherry pie filling

Preheat oven to 325 degrees F.

Scoop ice cream evenly into crust, alternating with layers of chocolate fudge sauce, beginning and ending with ice cream.

Spoon cherry pie filling over top layer of ice cream. Return to freezer until solid, about 3 hours. Serve frozen, using a large cake knife to cut pie.

Double-Chocolate Mousse

A mousse should be light in texture yet intensely flavored. The combination of pudding and chocolate fudge sauce does the trick.

SERVES 6.

1	box (4 servings) instant chocolate pudding mix
1/4	cup chocolate fudge sauce
2	cups heavy cream, very cold
2	tablespoons confectioners' sugar

Prepare pudding according to package directions, but stir in chocolate fudge sauce while mixing. Refrigerate until cold.

In bowl of electric mixer, combine cream and sugar. Beat until stiff, about 1½ minutes. Fold cold chocolate mixture into whipped cream. Spoon into dessert glasses or bowl and serve or chill up to 24 hours.

desserts

Lemon Curd Shortcake

Lemon curd is a rich butter-and-egg-based fruit spread that you'll use on everything from shortcake to crepes.

SERVES 6.

1	jar (8 to 10 ounces) lemon curd
1	container (8 ounces) frozen whipped topping
1	can (6 count) refrigerated biscuits
18	large strawberries

Combine lemon curd and half of the whipped topping.

Bake biscuits according to package directions and cool. Place one biscuit on each of 6 plates, and split in half. Top bottom half each with one-fourth of the curd mixture.

Slice all but 6 strawberries. Arrange sliced berries over curd. Close with top half of biscuits.

Top each biscuit with a generous dollop of remaining whipped topping. Place a whole strawberry over the cream. Serve immediately.

Extreme-Chocolate
Cream Cheese Brownies

Use your favorite brownie mix for this confection but avoid "extra-moist" products.

MAKES 20 BROWNIES.

1	box (19.8 ounces) dark-style chocolate fudge brownie mix
2	eggs
1/2	cup unsalted butter, melted
1	cup coarsely chopped walnuts
1	bar (3 ounces) bittersweet or semisweet chocolate, coarsely chopped
1	package (8 ounces) cream cheese, softened
1/4	cup sugar
1/4	teaspoon vanilla extract

Preheat oven to 325 degrees F.

In bowl of heavy-duty mixer, combine brownie mix, 1 egg, 1/3 cup water, and melted butter. Beat 1 minute. Stir in walnuts and chocolate. Spread in greased and floured 9-by-13-inch pan. Set aside.

In bowl of heavy-duty mixer, combine cream cheese, sugar, and remaining egg. Beat until light, about 1 minute, scraping down sides of bowl. Stir in vanilla.

Drop cream cheese batter by the heaping tablespoon over chocolate batter. Use a knife to swirl cream cheese into chocolate. Level off.

Bake for 35 minutes or until toothpick inserted 1 inch from edge of pan comes out clean.

Remove from oven. Cool completely, then cut.

Orange-Scented Marble Pound Cake

The traditional pound cake was named for the weight of the ingredients: 1 pound each of eggs, butter, and flour. Start with a mix, and you won't have the recipe weighing on you.

SERVES 12.

1	box (1 pound) pound cake mix
2	eggs
6	tablespoons milk
1	bar (3 ounces) bittersweet or semisweet chocolate, broken into bite-size pieces, melted
	Grated rind of 1 orange
1/4	cup orange juice

Preheat oven to 350 degrees F.

Place pound cake mix in bowl of electric mixer. Add eggs and milk. Beat at medium speed 2 minutes. Remove 2/3 cup batter and place in bowl. Stir in melted chocolate, beating well. Set aside.

ADD A TOUCH: Stir 1/2 cup chopped walnuts into the orange-flavored batter.

Add orange rind and orange juice to batter remaining in mixing bowl. Beat 2 minutes.

Grease bottom of 9-by-5-inch loaf pan. Spoon in orange pound cake batter. Drop chocolate batter over orange pound cake batter in dollops. Cut in chocolate layer with a knife to create marble effect. Level off.

Bake 55 to 60 minutes or until toothpick inserted near center comes out clean. Cool 15 minutes. Turn out onto rack, cool completely, and serve.

Kitchen Sink Cookies

Start with a chewy-style cookie mix and stir in your favorite flavorings. These big, chunky cookies are great for bag lunches.

MAKES 24 TO 30 COOKIES.

1	box (18 ounces) oatmeal or oatmeal raisin cookie mix*
1	egg, beaten
1/2	cup butter, softened
1	cup trail mix with nuts, dried fruit, and chocolate chips

Preheat oven to 350 degrees F.

In a bowl, beat together cookie mix, egg, and butter according to package directions. Stir in trail mix.

Drop batter by heaping tablespoon 2 inches apart onto ungreased cookie sheet. Bake 13 to 15 minutes or until lightly browned. Let cookies set on sheet 10 minutes. Remove to a wire rack to completely cool.

*If possible, look for a cookie mix that calls for an egg, plus butter or margarine, not vegetable oil.

Gooey Delicious Cookie Bars

These bars go into the oven looking like a mess but come out picture-perfect with golden coconut topping.

MAKES 20 BARS.

1/2	cup butter, melted
2	cups chocolate cookie crumbs from 1 box (15 ounces) chocolate cookie crumbs
1/2	cup milk chocolate chips
1/2	cup butterscotch chips
1	cup chopped walnuts
1	cup sweetened, flaked coconut
1	can (14 ounces) sweetened condensed milk

Preheat oven to 350 degrees F.

Stir together melted butter and cookie crumbs. Press into 9-by-13-inch baking pan.

Sprinkle on, in order, chocolate chips, butterscotch chips, walnuts, and coconut. Spoon condensed milk over all. Bake for 30 minutes.

Remove from oven. Top may still be sticky but will firm up as it cools.

Cut into bars while still warm. Allow to cool and set before serving.

ADD A TOUCH:
Top each serving with a scoop of vanilla ice cream.

Raspberry Fool

Choose your favorite fruit and yogurt combinations for this light dessert. Try bananas with blueberry or mixed berry yogurt, for example.

SERVES 4.

1	bag (12 ounces) frozen raspberries, thawed and drained if necessary
1/4	cup sugar, divided
1/4	cup whipping cream
1	container (6 ounces) lemon-flavored yogurt

In a bowl, toss together raspberries and 2 tablespoons sugar. Set aside.

Using an electric mixer, whip cream until soft peaks form. Gradually add remaining sugar. Continue beating until stiff.

Fold yogurt into cream. Gently fold raspberries into yogurt-cream. Spoon into serving bowl or individual glasses.

Chocolate-Mint Hot Fudge Sauce

Turn plain vanilla ice cream or store-bought pound cake into a special dessert by topping it with warm-from-the-stove sauce. Store any leftovers in the refrigerator up to 1 week.

MAKES ABOUT 1 CUP.

1	cup mint-flavored chocolate chips
1/4	cup half-and-half
1	tablespoon butter

Combine all ingredients in a small, heavy-bottomed saucepan. Heat over low heat, stirring frequently, until melted, about 5 minutes.

ADD A TOUCH:
Add 1 tablespoon light corn syrup while melting the chocolate for a fudge sauce with a slightly chewy texture that's very appealing.

Peanutty Brownies

MAKES 16 BROWNIES.

	Peanut butter frosting (follows)
1	box baked brownies in 9-inch square pan
1	cup miniature chocolate chips

Prepare peanut butter frosting. Spread over brownies. Sprinkle with chocolate chips. Cut into 16 squares. Refrigerate to store.

Peanut Butter Frosting

2/3	cup peanut butter
3	tablespoons butter
1	cup confectioners' sugar
1	tablespoon cream, half-and-half, or milk

In bowl of electric mixer, beat together all ingredients until mixture is light.

Strawberry Cheesecake

Vary the pie filling to include blueberry, cherry, or blackberry, and you'll never tire of this dessert.

SERVES 6 TO 8.

1	box (16 to 24 ounces) cheesecake mix
1	can (24 ounces) strawberry pie filling
1	tablespoon fresh lemon juice (optional)

Prepare cheesecake mix according to package directions. Bake according to package directions, but remove from oven 10 minutes early.

While cheesecake is baking, stir together strawberry pie filling and lemon juice.

Remove partially set cake from oven. Spread with strawberry topping. Place cheesecake on cookie sheet to catch any drips. Return to oven and bake 10 minutes. Remove cheesecake and chill 2 to 3 hours or until set.

Apple Breakfast Cake

Make this delicious and nourishing coffee cake for a weekend brunch or after-school snack. It also freezes well.

SERVES 9.

1	box (17.4 ounces) bran or oatmeal muffin mix
1	egg, beaten
1/4	cup butter
1 1/4	cups milk
1	apple, peeled and finely diced

ADD A TOUCH:
Add 1 cup chopped walnuts to the batter.

Preheat oven to 350 degrees F.

Place muffin mix in large bowl. Add any flavoring mixes that come with the product.

In a small bowl, beat together egg, butter, and milk. Add to muffin mix. Stir in apple. Do not beat.

Spoon into greased 8-inch square pan. Bake 45 to 50 minutes or until cake is completely done in center. Remove from oven and serve.

desserts

Butterscotch Bread Pudding

1   package (3 ounces) ready-to-cook butterscotch pudding
3   cups milk
1   tablespoon butter
2   tablespoons brown sugar
2   eggs
6   slices white bread

Preheat oven to 300 degrees F.

Combine pudding, milk, butter, and brown sugar in small saucepan. Cook over low heat until mixture is simmering.

Beat eggs together in small bowl. Pour about ½ cup milk mixture over eggs and stir well. Pour egg mixture back into pot. Cook over low heat until thick and smooth.

Meanwhile, toast bread. Cut each slice into 3 strips.

Arrange half the bread on greased 8-inch square pan. Pour on half the pudding. Cover with remaining bread and remaining pudding.

Bake for 45 minutes or until pudding is set. Remove from oven and let set another 5 minutes and serve while warm.

Nut Crescents

Rugalach, a flaky, rich European pastry, is the inspiration for this cookie.

MAKES 16 CRESCENTS.

1	box (15 ounces) refrigerated piecrusts, 2 crusts to a package
1/4	cup butter, divided
1	teaspoon ground cinnamon
1/2	cup sugar
1	cup chopped pecans

ADD A TOUCH:
Add 1 cup dried cherries along with the nuts.

Preheat oven to 375 degrees F.

Work with one crust at a time. Unfold on work surface. Brush crust with 1 tablespoon butter.

Combine cinnamon and sugar. Sprinkle 2 tablespoons of sugar mixture on crust. Sprinkle on 1/2 cup chopped nuts.

Using a sharp knife or pizza wheel, cut crust into 8 wedges. Starting from wide end, roll up to the point. Place on greased cookie sheet. Press in any filling that falls out.

Repeat with remaining crust and filling. You should have 2 tablespoons butter and 1/4 cup sugar mixture remaining.

Brush crescents with remaining butter and sprinkle with remaining cinnamon-sugar. Bake for 18 minutes or until golden. Remove from oven and serve.

desserts

Oatmeal, Pear, and Cranberry Crumble

This old-fashioned dessert is modernized by using a cookie mix in place of the traditional rolled-oat toppings.

SERVES 8.

1	can (1 pound) pear slices, drained
1	rounded cup dried, sweetened cranberries
1	box (1 pound, 1.5 ounces) oatmeal cookie mix
1/2	cup butter, melted
1	cup chopped walnuts

Preheat oven to 375 degrees F.

Combine pears and cranberries in 9-by-13-inch baking dish.

In a bowl, toss together cookie mix, butter, and nuts. Sprinkle over fruit in even, thick layer. Bake 30 minutes or until topping is browned. Remove from oven and serve.

ADD A TOUCH:
Serve over vanilla
ice cream.

Million-Dollar Popcorn

Serve this sweet treat as a dessert, snack, or party nibble. For the best crunchy texture, use freshly popped popcorn.

SERVES 20.

10	cups popped microwave popcorn, divided
1	cup whole almonds
3/4	cup butterscotch chips
3/4	cup milk chocolate chips
	Salt

Combine 5 cups popcorn and nuts and spread out on cookie sheet.

Place butterscotch chips in microwave-safe bowl. Microwave on medium heat for 1 minute or until chips melt. Drizzle over popcorn and nuts. Set aside for 5 minutes. Add remaining popcorn, but don't mix.

Melt chocolate as directed for butterscotch chips. Drizzle chocolate over plain popcorn. Gently toss two layers together to mix. Season lightly with salt. Refrigerate mixture for 1 hour.

Break into pieces and serve. May store in covered container in refrigerator up to 3 days.

desserts

Lime Wafers

For convenience, shape the cookie dough as directed, then freeze on a cookie sheet. Store in a plastic bag in the freezer and bake within 3 months.

MAKES 14 WAFERS.

6	tablespoons confectioners' sugar
1 1/3	cups piecrust mix
1	tablespoon butter
2	tablespoons lime juice

Preheat oven to 300 degrees F.

In bowl of electric mixer, combine confectioners' sugar, piecrust mix, and butter. Beat 30 seconds. Add lime juice and blend until dough holds together.

Scoop out dough and roll into balls the size of a quarter. Place on greased cookie sheet. Flatten balls to 1/3-inch thickness. Bake for 18 to 20 minutes. Remove from oven and serve.

ADD A TOUCH:
Dust cookies with confectioners' sugar while they're warm from the oven.

Coconut Cream Bars

Use a coconut cream or even pistachio instant-pudding mix to make this update of coconut cream pie.

MAKES 9 BARS.

1	box (11 ounces) piecrust mix (2$^1/_3$ cups)
$^1/_4$	cup confectioners' sugar
$^1/_4$	cup quick-cooking oats
2	tablespoons butter
$^1/_4$	cup milk
	Coconut Filling (follows)

Preheat oven to 350 degrees F.

In a bowl, combine piecrust mix, confectioners' sugar, oats, butter, and milk. Blend ingredients until crumbly. Press into greased 9-inch square pan. Bake 12 minutes. Remove and set aside to cool.

Prepare Coconut Filling (below). Pour over crust. Chill 2 hours. Cut into squares and serve.

Coconut Filling

2	boxes (3.4 ounces each) French vanilla instant pudding mix
2	cups milk
$^1/_2$	cup whipping or heavy cream
1	cup sweetened, shredded coconut

In bowl of electric mixer, combine pudding, milk, and cream. Beat 3 minutes or until thick. Fold in coconut.

Chocolate Pudding Squares

You loved S'mores as a child. As an adult, you'll love this double-chocolate variation.

MAKES 9 SQUARES.

1/4	cup butter, melted
1 1/4	cups chocolate cookie crumbs from 1 box (15 ounces) chocolate cookie crumbs
1/4	cup sugar
2	boxes (3.9 ounces each) instant chocolate pudding mix
2	cups milk
1/2	cup whipping or heavy cream
1	cup miniature marshmallows

Preheat oven to 350 degrees F.

Combine butter, cookie crumbs, and sugar in a 9-inch square pan. Pat down to form a crust. Bake for 6 to 8 minutes. Remove pan and set aside to cool.

In bowl of electric mixer, combine pudding, milk, and cream. Beat at high speed 3 minutes or until very thick. Spread over crust. Sprinkle on marshmallows. Chill 2 to 3 hours or until set.

Chocolate Chip Ice Cream Sandwiches

For a party, set out stacks of cookies and cartons of ice cream and let guests create their own sandwich combinations.

MAKES 8 SANDWICHES.

16	(3- to 4-inch diameter) chocolate-chip cookies
2	cartons (1 pint each) vanilla fudge ice cream, slightly softened
1	cup miniature chocolate chips

ADD A TOUCH:
Stir nuts, mini marshmallows, and dried cherries into the ice cream before spreading it on the cookies.

Arrange 8 cookies on a work surface.

Spread ½ cup ice cream on each of 8 cookies, creating a level layer. Top with a second cookie to make a sandwich.

Spread chips on a platter. Hold sandwiches filling side down and coat ice cream with chips. Serve immediately or return to freezer.

Dulce de Leche Fondue

Fondues are back. Get the pot out of the attic and heat up dulce de leche, a caramel topping, as an instant dip for fruit.

SERVES 4.

1	jar (12 ounces) dulce de leche milk caramel topping
2	apples or bananas, or one of each
1/4	cup miniature chocolate chips
1/4	cup sweetened shredded coconut
1/4	cup chopped pecans
1/4	cup chocolate-coated toffee bar chips

Place caramel topping in microwave-safe bowl or in fondue pot over heat source. For a microwave, heat at medium heat for 45 seconds or until warm. For a fondue pot, heat for 3 to 5 minutes.

Core and seed apples. Cut into 1-inch chunks. Peel bananas, if used, and cut into 1-inch chunks.

Place fruit pieces in a bowl. Place chips, coconut, nuts, and toffee chips in small separate bowls.

To serve, dip fruit into caramel, then roll in topping of choice.

Cocoa and Grand Marnier Strawberries

Look for Driscoll or other showstopper strawberries to use in this deceptively simple dessert.

SERVES 4.

16	jumbo red strawberries, unhulled
1/4	cup Grand Marnier
1	envelope hot cocoa or hot chocolate mix

Wash berries and pat dry.

Place Grand Marnier in shallow bowl.

Pour hot cocoa mix in second bowl.

To serve, dip berries in Grand Marnier, then roll in cocoa mixture to coat.

Créme Brulée

This dessert, the rage of trendy restaurants, is simply custard with a brown sugar topping that melts to form a crisp shell.

SERVES 4.

1	box (2.9 ounces) custard mix
¹/₄	cup brown sugar

Prepare custard mix according to package directions. Pour into 4 custard cups. Refrigerate until completely cold, about 3 hours.

Sprinkle 2 teaspoons brown sugar over each serving.

Place custard cups on cookie sheet. Place under broiler about 2 inches from heat for 30 seconds or until sugar melts. Remove from heat. Let stand 10 minutes or until sugar firms up into shell.

Snowballs

You'd never know from the plain exterior that a melted delicious chocolate morsel waits inside this cookie.

MAKES 26 TO 28 COOKIES.

1	box (1 pound, 1.5 ounces) sugar cookie mix
1/2	cup butter, melted
1	egg, beaten
1/4	cup flour
26	to 28 foil-wrapped chocolate candies (like Hershey's Kisses)
1/4	cup confectioners' sugar

Preheat oven to 325 degrees F.

Combine cookie mix, butter, egg, and flour in a bowl. Stir to form a dough. Shape into balls by the heaping tablespoonful.

Unwrap chocolate candies. Place one chocolate in center of each scoop of dough. Work dough around chocolate to cover. Place on ungreased cookie sheet. Repeat with remaining dough. Bake 18 to 20 minutes or until cookies are set and lightly browned.

Remove from oven and dust with confectioners' sugar while still warm.

desserts

Impossible Chocolate Cake

This classic pudding cake found its way from the back of a box of biscuit mix into many cooks' permanent collections. It is at its most delicious served warm from the oven

SERVES 8.

1	cup biscuit mix
1	cup sugar, divided
1/3	cup plus 3 tablespoons unsweetened cocoa
1/2	cup milk
1	teaspoon vanilla extract
1 2/3	cups hot water

Preheat oven to 325 degrees F.

In 9-inch square greased cake pan, stir together biscuit mix, 1/2 cup sugar, and 3 tablespoons cocoa.

Combine milk and vanilla and stir into biscuit mixture to make a batter.

Combine remaining sugar and cocoa. Sprinkle over batter in even layer. Pour on hot water.

Bake for 40 minutes. Cake layer will form on top with pudding on the bottom. Remove from oven and serve.

from your bakery

Bread-Machine Sour Cream & Onion Bread

Sour cream produces a tender texture and tangy sourdough flavor in bread.

MAKES 1 LOAF.

1/2	cup sour cream
2	tablespoons onion soup mix
1	box (15.4 ounces) white bread mix
1	envelope (.25 ounces) yeast for bread machine

Following instructions of bread machine, place sour cream, 1/2 cup water, and onion soup mix in container of bread machine.

Add bread mix. Sprinkle on yeast. Select basic setting on machine. Follow machine directions, checking the dough during initial mixing. If dough is stiff, add an additional 2 to 4 tablespoons water. When machine is finished, remove from bread machine and serve.

Streusel-Topped Chocolate Muffins

The contrast of a crunchy chocolate topping and the tender crumb of the chocolate muffin makes this recipe special.

MAKES 12 MUFFINS.

1/4	cup chocolate cookie crumbs from 15-ounce box chocolate cookie crumbs
1	tablespoon butter, cut into small pieces
1/4	cup chopped walnuts
1	box (1 pound, 2.25 ounces) chocolate muffin mix
1	egg, beaten

ADD A TOUCH:
Fold 1/2 cup mini chocolate chips into muffin batter.

Preheat oven to 400 degrees F.

To make streusel topping, spoon crumbs into a small bowl. Cut in butter until crumbly. Stir in walnuts. Set aside.

Pour muffin mix into a bowl. Add 1 cup water and egg and stir just to mix.

Grease muffin tin. Spoon in batter. Do not fill to top. Sprinkle 1 tablespoon topping over each muffin. Bake 18 to 22 minutes or until toothpick inserted near center comes out clean. Remove from oven and serve.

from your bakery

Blueberry Coffee Cake

Sour cream is a tenderizer that gives this coffee cake its delicate texture.

SERVES 9.

2/3	cup sugar
1	egg
1/2	cup milk
2	tablespoons butter
1	teaspoon vanilla extract
1/2	cup sour cream
2	cups biscuit mix
1 1/2	cups fresh or frozen blueberries

Preheat oven to 350 degrees F.

In a bowl, combine sugar, egg, milk, butter, and vanilla extract. Beat 30 seconds. Stir in sour cream. Beat in biscuit mix. Add blueberries and gently fold in.

Spoon into greased and floured 8-inch square pan. Bake 45 to 50 minutes. Remove from oven and serve.

Toffee Scones

Serve this cross between a tender cookie and a muffin for an afternoon snack or with Sunday brunch.

MAKES 4 SCONES.

1¹/₄	cups biscuit mix
1	tablespoon sugar
2	tablespoons butter, cut in small pieces
¹/₄	cup milk
¹/₄	cup chocolate-toffee chips
	Flour for dusting

Preheat oven to 400 degrees F.

In bowl of food processor, combine biscuit mix and sugar. Add butter chunks and turn machine on and off to cut butter into biscuit mix. Add milk and process just enough to moisten. Stir in chips and process just to incorporate.

Remove dough from food processor onto lightly floured board. Pat into one disk ³/₄ inch high. Cut with 2 ¹/₂-inch round cookie cutters forming 4 scones. Rework scraps but don't handle any more than necessary.

Place scones on greased cookie sheet. Bake 12 to 14 minutes until high and golden. Remove from oven and serve.

Sausage Pinwheels

For fresh-from-the-oven morning pinwheels, assemble this dish the night before and refrigerate.

MAKES 8 PINWHEELS.

1	apple, cored, seeded, and finely chopped
1	pound maple-flavored sausage
1	box (15.4 ounces) country white bread mix for use in bread machine

In 12-inch skillet, combine apple and sausage. Brown together, breaking up sausage with back of spoon, about 10 minutes. Pour off fat.

Meanwhile, prepare bread mix according to package directions. Set bread machine on "dough setting." Remove when bread machine signals.

Roll dough into 11-by-14-inch rectangle. Spread sausage mixture over dough, leaving 1-inch border. Roll up tightly from long side to create 14-inch log. Cut into 8 equal portions.

Preheat oven to 350 degrees F.

ADD A TOUCH:
Sprinkle 1 table-spoon grated Parmesan cheese over each pinwheel before baking.

Place rolls cut side up in greased 9-inch square pan. Cover with towel and set aside in warm place 30 minutes. Bake rolls 35 to 40 minutes or until golden. Remove from oven and serve.

Herbed Dinner Rolls

A butter and oregano glaze colors dinner rolls golden brown and fills the kitchen with an alluring aroma.

MAKES 9 ROLLS.

9	brown-and-serve dinner rolls
1/4	cup butter or margarine
1/2	teaspoon crushed, dried oregano

Place dinner rolls on a cookie sheet.

In a small pot, combine butter and oregano. Melt together.

Brush butter mixture generously over rolls and heat according to package directions. Remove from oven and serve warm.

Corny Cornbread

Cornbread tastes best right from the oven. Use any leftovers as a stuffing for pork chops.

SERVES 9.

1	box (8.5 ounces) cornbread mix
1	egg, beaten
1/3	cup milk
1	cup frozen or canned corn kernels

Preheat oven to 400 degrees F.

Spoon cornbread mix into a bowl. Add egg and milk. Stir briefly, just to mix. Stir in corn kernels.

Spread mixture in greased 8-inch square dish. Bake 20 minutes or until toothpick inserted near center comes out clean. Remove from oven and serve.

ADD A TOUCH:
Stir in 1 can (4 ounces) diced green chiles, drained.

Southwestern Cheddar Scones

Scones are richer than muffins or biscuits because of their higher fat content. They're also more crumbly, so handle carefully.

MAKES 8 SCONES.

1	box (8.5 ounces) corn muffin mix
1/4	cup (1/2 stick) butter, melted
1	egg, beaten
1	can (4 ounces) diced chiles, drained
1	cup shredded sharp Cheddar cheese

Preheat oven to 400 degrees F.

Pour muffin mix into a medium-size bowl.

In a small bowl, stir together butter and egg. Stir in canned chiles. Spoon butter mixture into muffin mix. Stir in cheese.

Using a 1/4-cup measure, scoop out batter onto greased cookie sheet, leaving at least 2 inches between scones.

Bake for 13 to 15 minutes or until scones are golden brown and firm to the touch. Remove from oven. Let sit on cookie sheet 5 minutes, then remove to wire rack. Serve warm.

from your bakery

Lemon-Glazed Poppy Seed Bread

Serve this tea bread as an afternoon snack, as a brunch accompaniment, or even as a dessert.

SERVES 10.

1	box (15.8 ounces) lemon poppy seed muffin mix
1	cup milk
1	egg
¹/₄	cup butter, melted
	Lemon Glaze (follows)

Preheat oven to 350 degrees F.

Place muffin mix in bowl.

In small bowl, combine milk, egg, and butter. Stir. Add milk mixture to muffin mix. Stir briefly. Do not beat.

Spoon into greased and floured 9-by-5-inch loaf pan. Bake 50 to 55 minutes or until toothpick inserted in center comes out clean. Remove from oven. Let stand 5 minutes while making Lemon Glaze (below).

Turn loaf out onto wire rack. Top with glaze while still hot. Let cool completely before slicing and serving.

Lemon Glaze

¹/₃	cup confectioners' sugar, sifted if lumpy
	Grated rind of 1 lemon
1	tablespoon lemon juice

In a bowl, stir together all ingredients. Mix until thickened and completely smooth.

Cheese-Pepper Croissants

Don't be tempted to buy full-fat crescent rolls for this delicious croissant. The reduced-fat version tastes better when filled with cheese.

MAKES 8 CROISSANTS.

1	cup grated Parmesan cheese
1/2	teaspoon coarsely ground black pepper
1	package (15.5 ounces) reduced-fat crescent rolls (8 rolls)

Preheat oven to 375 degrees F.

Combine cheese and pepper in a bowl. Stir well.

On a work surface, unroll crescent rolls with point facing away from you. Sprinkle 2 tablespoons cheese mixture on each crescent roll. Roll tightly from wide end to point. Place each roll, point side down, on ungreased cookie sheet. Repeat to use all rolls and cheese mixture.

Bake for 12 to 14 minutes or until golden brown. Remove from oven and serve warm.

menus and recipes for entertaining

a night in seville

Olive Bruschetta

Look for a jar of olive pesto, caponata, or coarse olive paste to top this robust appetizer.

SERVES 8.

1	box (11.25 ounces) frozen Texas garlic toast (8 slices)
1/2	cup olive pesto
1/2	cup grated fontina, Asiago, or mozzarella cheese

ADD A TOUCH:
Vary the flavor using olive, tomato, or red pepper pesto.

Preheat oven to 425 degrees F.

Arrange garlic toast on cookie sheet. Bake for 3 minutes.

Remove from oven. Spread 1 tablespoon pesto on each toast slice. Sprinkle each slice with 1 tablespoon cheese. Return to oven and bake another 5 minutes or until cheese melts. Remove from oven and serve.

Gazpacho

This cold, refreshing soup depends on tangy-sweet tomatoes for its taste. If vine-ripened fresh tomatoes aren't in season, switch to canned ones.

SERVES 4 TO 6.

1	box (1 quart) tomato juice, chilled
1	cucumber, peeled and coarsely chopped
2	scallions, trimmed and coarsely chopped
2	medium tomatoes, cored and coarsely chopped
1/4	teaspoon crushed red pepper flakes*
1	tablespoon white wine vinegar
1/2	teaspoon salt
1/2	teaspoon pepper

Pour tomato juice into pitcher.

Place all remaining ingredients in bowl of food processor fitted with steel blade. Turn food processor on and off in quick bursts to finely chop vegetables. Add to tomato juice. Serve immediately or chill up to 4 hours.

*1/4 teaspoon crushed red pepper flakes is mildly hot; 1/2 teaspoon is quite steamy.

Paella

This classic Spanish skillet dish of seafood, chicken, and sausage gets its robust flavor from lean, highly seasoned poultry sausages available in most supermarkets.

SERVES 6.

1	tablespoon vegetable oil
1	red bell pepper, cored, seeded, and diced
1	package (8 ounces) thinly sliced pepperoni
1	package (12 ounces) medium, raw, peeled, deveined shrimp
1	box (8 ounces) New Orleans–style yellow rice

Heat oil in 12-inch skillet. Add bell pepper and sauté 5 minutes over medium heat. Add pepperoni and brown 1 minute. Add 2 cups water. Bring to a boil. Stir in shrimp and rice.

Cover skillet. Reduce heat to low and simmer 30 minutes or until rice is tender and liquid is absorbed. Remove from heat and serve.

Chocolate Nut Squares

Think of pecan pie, then add even more nuts and chocolate chips, and you've got a scrumptious dessert.

SERVES 8.

1/2	box (11 ounces) piecrust mix, 1 1/3 cups
2	tablespoons confectioners' sugar
	Chocolate Nut Filling (follows)

Preheat oven to 350 degrees F.

In a bowl, stir together piecrust mix and confectioners' sugar. Add 2 to 3 tablespoons cold water. Stir with fork until dough sticks together.

Pat dough into greased 8-inch square pan. Bake for 10 minutes or until set.

Remove from oven. Prepare Chocolate Nut Filling (below). Pour over crust. Return to oven and bake another 30 minutes or until set. Remove from oven and serve.

Chocolate Nut Filling

1/2	cup each chopped pecans, almonds, and walnuts
3/4	cup light corn syrup
1/3	cup brown sugar
3	tablespoons melted butter
2	large eggs, beaten
1/8	teaspoon salt
1/2	cup chocolate chips

Combine ingredients in bowl and stir well.

menus and recipes for entertaining

spring brunch

Viennese Brunch Café

Experiment with different liqueurs, such as Grand Marnier or crème de menthe, to add punch to a coffee mix.

SERVES 4.

1/2	cup Vienna-flavored coffee mix
1/4	cup amaretto
1/2	cup whipped cream or whipped topping

Bring 1 quart water to a boil.

Measure 2 tablespoons coffee mix into each of 4 heat-proof mugs. Pour 1 cup boiling hot water into each mug. Add 1 tablespoon amaretto to each mug. Top each mug with 2 tablespoons whipped cream. Serve immediately.

ADD A TOUCH:
Set out bowls of whipped cream and chocolate chips and let guests top their own coffee creations.

Asparagus Omelet with Leek Sauce

Fresh vegetables and a rich sauce turn eggs into an indulgent brunch entrée. Flavor eggs with chopped spinach or broccoli if you prefer.

SERVES 4.

1	box (10 ounces) frozen chopped asparagus
8	eggs
1/4	cup grated Parmesan cheese
1	tablespoon butter
	Leek Sauce (follows)

Cook asparagus according to package directions. Drain and set aside.

In a bowl, beat eggs with cheese. Melt butter in 12-inch skillet. Pour in egg mixture and cook over medium heat 5 minutes or until partially set. Sprinkle asparagus pieces over omelet. Cook 3 more minutes or until set.

Meanwhile, prepare Leek Sauce (below). To serve, cut omelet into 4 wedges. Top each with a portion of Leek Sauce. Serve extra sauce on the side.

Leek Sauce

1	box (1.8 ounces) leek soup, dip, and recipe mix
2	cups milk

Combine leek soup mix with milk in small saucepan. Bring to a boil. Reduce heat to medium and simmer 1 to 2 minutes or until sauce is the consistency of cake batter.

Gooey Pecan Buns

These finger-lickin' buns require little effort. Use a deep-dish pan or place the pan on a cookie sheet, or the filling may bubble over.

SERVES 10.

10	refrigerated brown-and-serve dinner rolls
2	tablespoons melted butter
1/2	cup chopped pecans
1/2	cup chopped raisins
1/2	cup butterscotch ice-cream topping

Preheat oven to 350 degrees F.

Place rolls in large bowl. Toss rolls with melted butter, pecans, and raisins. Add butterscotch ice-cream topping. Stir well.

Place rolls and coating mixture in well-greased, deep, 9-inch round pan. Bake 5 to 10 minutes or until rolls are golden.

Remove from oven and immediately turn rolls upside down onto serving dish.

ADD A TOUCH:
Stir in 1/4 teaspoon ground cinnamon with the melted butter.

buffet dinners for friends

Glazed Baked Ham

Make a double batch of the spicy-sweet chutney glaze and use the leftovers as a spread for ham sandwiches.

SERVES 12 TO 18.

1	smoked, fully cooked spiral-cut ham (6 pounds)
1	cup mango chutney
2	tablespoons honey mustard

Preheat oven to 325 degrees F.

Place ham in shallow roasting pan. Cover with foil. Bake for 1 hour.

Combine chutney and mustard. Glaze ham with mixture. Bake another 30 minutes. Remove from oven and serve.

Barbecued Sweet Potatoes

Roasting concentrates the sugars and creates a crisp outer shell for sweet potato wedges.

SERVES 12.

4	large sweet potatoes
1	package (1.6 ounces) Buffalo wings seasoning mix
1/4	cup olive oil

Preheat oven to 400 degrees F.

Wash potatoes. Halve widthwise. Cut each half into 6 wedges, 12 per potato.

Pour seasoning mix into a bag. Add potato wedges and shake to coat.

Spread potatoes in shallow roasting pan. Drizzle with oil. Roast 20 minutes, turn potatoes over, and roast another 15 minutes or until tender. Remove from oven and serve.

Peach Crépes

You'll find packaged crépes in supermarket produce sections.
Choose the traditional round or easy-to-fill square-shaped crépes.

SERVES 12.

6	tablespoons butter
3	cans (16 ounces each) peach or apple pie filling
12	brown-and-serve crépes

ADD A TOUCH:

Top crépes with

vanilla ice cream.

Melt butter in large, nonstick pot. Add filling and heatg 3 minutes.

Assemble crépes by arranging 1 crepe on a work surface. Top with about ¼ cup filling mixture along one side of crepe. Roll up to enclose. Repeat with remaining crépes.

Arrange on platter. Top with remaining filling.

D

International Conversion Chart

These are not exact equivalents: they have been slightly rounded to make measuring easier.

LIQUID MEASUREMENTS

American	Imperial	Metric	Australian
2 tablespoons (1 oz.)	1 fl. oz.	30 ml	1 tablespoon
1/4 cup (2 oz.)	2 fl. oz.	60 ml	2 tablespoons
1/3 cup (3 oz.)	3 fl. oz.	80 ml	1/4 cup
1/4 cup (4 oz.)	4 fl. oz.	125 ml	1/3 cup
2/3 cup (5 oz.)	5 fl. oz.	165 ml	1/2 cup
3/4 cup (6 oz.)	6 fl. oz.	185 ml	2/3 cup
1 cup (8 oz.)	8 fl. oz.	250 ml	3/4 cup

SPOON MEASUREMENTS

American	Metric
1/4 teaspoon	1 ml
1/2 teaspoon	2 ml
1 teaspoon	5 ml
1 tablespoon	15 ml

WEIGHTS

US/UK	Metric
1 oz.	30 grams (g)
2 oz.	60 g
4 oz. (1/4 lb)	125 g
5 oz. (1/3 lb)	155 g
6 oz.	185 g
7 oz.	220 g
8 oz. (1/2 lb)	250 g
10 oz.	315 g
12 oz. (3/4 lb)	375 g
14 oz.	440 g
16 oz. (1 lb)	500 g
2 lbs	1 kg

OVEN TEMPERATURES

Farenheit	Centigrade	Gas
250	120	1/4
300	150	2
325	160	3
350	180	4
375	190	5
400	200	6
450	230	8